KING HENRY IV
Part One

CONDITIONS OF SALE

This book shall not, by way of trade or otherwise, be lent, re-sold, hired out or otherwise circulated without the publisher's prior consent in any form of binding or cover other than that in which it is published and without a similar condition including this condition being imposed on the subsequent purchaser. The book is published at a net price, and is supplied subject to the Publishers Association Standard Conditions of Sale registered under the Restrictive Trade Practices Act, 1956.

GLOBE . SOUTHWARKE .

WILLIAM SHAKESPEARE

KING HENRY IV
Part One

Introduction by
ROGER PLANCHON

PAN BOOKS LTD
LONDON

Published 1972 by Pan Books Ltd,
33 Tothill Street, London, SW1.

ISBN 0 330 23163 4

ACKNOWLEDGEMENTS

Pan Books wishes to thank J. M. Dent & Sons for permission to use the authoritative text of the New Temple
Shakespeare, edited by M. R. Ridley; The Folio Society
for permission to use the Introduction by Roger Planchon
and the Glossary compiled by Miss Jean Rook; Times News-
papers Ltd for permission to reproduce the illustrations of
King Henry IV, *Falstaff*, and *Mistress Quickly*; the Trustees of
the British Museum for permission to reproduce the
Frontispiece, from the Pennant Collection; the Governors of the
Royal Shakespeare Theatre (Art Gallery) for permission to
reproduce the Flower portrait of *William Shakespeare*.

The following artists were responsible for cover and
character illustrations: *Cover*, showing *Prince Hal* and *Falstaff*,
by Alan Lee; *King Henry IV* by Alex Jaw Dokimov; *Falstaff*
by Charles Raymond; *Mistress Quickly* by Barbosa; *Glendower*
by Michael Leonard.

Printed and bound in England by
Hazell Watson & Viney Ltd,
Aylesbury, Bucks

Introduction

I recommend you to skip the preface, leap (poetically) on to a horse, and set off in pursuit of those great feudal figures as they slaver with fury in a last fling before tipping over.

The Renaissance knew how to convince us that individuals were men formed on a grand scale, that the popes of Rome were top people and that the smallest petty king would swallow a murder or an incest for his breakfast. But in *Henry IV* there are no monsters, there is no Incarnate Evil; even the angels have withdrawn. The characters are men who are at once simpler and more complicated; Hotspur, for instance, in his dealings with Lady Percy, might lead us to think that they were complete misogynists. The ladies come off very badly. Nobody pays any attention to one of them; the gallic unintelligibilities of the other are not understood. The huge knights are well depicted. It is an extensive gallery; look at that old sorcerer in armour, Glendower. Time has not flaked the paintings. Read the play.

This is an historical chronicle where every detail lives. The stage gets breathing space; we move from the waxed paving stones of a throne room to the smears of stale vomit in the backyard of a brothel. That is no inconsiderable matter. The bourgeois drawing-rooms of our modern plays, with their psychological interior decorations, smell stuffy by comparison with this mad gallop from one castle to another across whole provinces in order to rush to the slaughter-house: the frantic and ceremonious duel of the final act.

Less stuffy than *Richard III* or *King John*, *Henry IV* is an enormous pleasure. Each of its characters juggles his words, gets drunk on them and is caught up in the action just as in the other histories; a kingdom is sold at auction, but with enjoyment and in a more undisciplined and, in fact, much more intelligent form of construction.

Today the French are making the novel undergo a starvation cure, and they disapprove of this play for its variety of episodes. In the seventeenth century they stuffed the theatre into a corset.

This unfortunate precedent prevents them from appreciating the pleasures of a symphonic, baroque method of construction. I have been convinced by certain English commentators that the French spirit has done great damage here.

An ordinary play lasts three or four hours; here you have twice as much. The action is sketched out upon a stage whose boards measure ten metres by ten, and then deployed across the vastest imaginary space. The whole span, as one can feel it with its rallentandos and its dramatic accelerations, is confined in this trivial handful of hours of clock-time. It is like those peasant banquets where you have to swallow two immense soups one after the other. Bad luck on the sensitive. The outstanding pleasure of *Henry IV* lies in this joy, in this manhandling of time and space, in this lack of restraint.

Theatrical dialogue is a *matière* in the sense in which the term is used in modern painting. Squeezed out of the tube, it does not serve to define the problem, but hardens to fix the nature and contours of human beings caught up in a particular action. Conflict of ideas abstracts the character; the course of the action and the *matière* of the dialogue give him a solid base. Shakespeare makes use of all the verbal ironmongery of the tournaments, of courtly love and of knightly jousting. He turns it into honey by distilling the poetry from it. Clad in the armour of this rhetoric the Falstaffs, Henrys and Hotspurs come forward for a tournament in which words are pointed and break off like lances. In order to enjoy the story you must like paddling in this verbal compost, where part of our childhood comes back to us . . . You must enjoy those long speeches which Shakespeare constructed in poetic form in order to achieve greater opacity. The average speech in the theatre develops an argument, but these long speeches of Shakespeare's are arguments whose words radiate outwards and explode. I find myself appreciating the substantial difference between unreeling and radiation, between the linear and the circular expression of ideas.

The fact that my English is rudimentary will explain this naïve approach, but I believe in it.

This immense rhetoric, this perfection of expression became actual reality; this poetic flowering, the history of a nation. Historians may produce precise details and corrections in order to discredit the version of history given here, but they will never be able to convince us; they would need to write with the freshness and fire of the young Percy.

So there is *Henry IV*, a poet's splendid meditation on history. Civil war has turned a kingdom into a pigsty where the pigs battle for provinces because they wish to know where legitimacy resides. Within his deepest self, inside his palace, Henry IV tries to hunt it down; it is parodied in the taverns; it is chased along the roads; on the battlefields armies, those splendid hounds of morality, clash noisily to establish by force of arms that power is in the hands of the usurper or that legitimacy will be able to beat down any rival.

From our evening papers we learn that in Berlin, in Formosa, in Saigon and so forth it is still a question of the legitimacy of power . . . Commentators have established the pattern from the chronicles: the usurper goes from treachery to treachery, seizes power and is then crushed so that morality can triumph. In *Henry IV* the usurper triumphs and this reversal of things makes morality seem somewhat ambiguous. It is well known how much commentators have written in order to reassert the play's morality, but the ambiguity of it is all the more striking for that.

Bolingbroke dreams of a crusade to a distant Jerusalem and, when he has to die in his bed, chooses a dim room of his palace which is named 'Jerusalem'. Is that divine will? Or an esoteric symbol? Or a final ironic point? . . . Your personal philosophy will not give you the key here, but it will allow you to write a thesis on the divine character of royal functions in Shakespeare's works or on the way in which his figures exploit this divinity in order to justify royalty. Henry IV, for instance, cannot undertake this crusade, since he is a usurper, or else he only dreamt of it in order to 'busy giddy minds with foreign quarrels'. His regrets, his doubts, his repentance in that case are only the psychological justifications of a workable policy, and accordingly without

9

interest: his sincerity is only a measure of his degree of mystification. According to which thesis you write you can say either that it is important for the symbolism of this monarcho-religious morality that Henry should kill Hotspur, or else that Shakespeare has here condensed the historical transition from feudalism to monarchy, showing that the establishment of a centralizing monarchy depended on the disappearance of the great feudal figures. Don't we, in fact, see that the second revolt (the Archbishop of York's) is a parody of the first—I suggest that a quotation from Hegel should be introduced supporting the thesis that historical events happen twice, once as tragedy and the second time as farce—and don't we learn when the revolt has been crushed that the national war against the French is about to follow? (This is the place for various quotations about history and its tricks: see how we have moved from a mystical crusade for the 'liberation of Jerusalem' to a common-or-garden war.)

It has been said that Shakespeare was providing a moral solution to a basically political problem, but in this case the traditional plot (triumph of the usurper followed by his downfall) takes an unexpected turning, so that it might be truer to say that Shakespeare solved the moral problem by political means. This twist casts a debatable light on a certain morality. Shakespeare stages its trial in such a way that we needn't be bored by the speeches for and against, and are not asked to condemn anybody. The monarchy is victorious and feudalism chokes itself in its outdated attempts at revolt. The spectators are the jury; they have nothing to judge but only to understand; they are spectators because they must learn that they are also actors.

This is where we should bring on the obese Falstaff, or rather allow him to sprawl across the page. When accused he is his own counsel and his plea is so brilliant as to turn him into the prosecutor-general who finally overcomes the spirit of solemnity. But isn't he, too, marvellously ambiguous? 'As an individual he is negativity itself; it is as a representative of the people that he is a source of liberation.' An amusing contradiction which should be followed down all its twists and turns.

When we held a public discussion on the play a Villeurbanne worker who was visiting the theatre for the first time in his life summed up the plot on the following lines: the boss's son has broken with his family, knocks about the night-clubs a bit, then joins the army to go and fight in Indo-China; he comes back and takes over the factory where, his dad having died, he proves a rather stricter master, not scrupling to have his own friends put in prison.

This is a good summary and quite as eloquent as the fifth act's monologue on honour. It is a shocking summary, just the kind Falstaff himself might have made. It expresses a refreshing popular sanity. Falstaff must rise again; our own sanity demands it. Those who take him off to the Fleet once more must be seen as a menace.

This epic also contains a secret inner meaning which ought to please the archaeologists of the psyche. Does it not show the long-drawn-out return of a son to his father? The old 'struggle' of which Kafka spoke? Another version of the old legend of the frustrated father? The father dreams of having a good son; what he sees is a debauched wreck and his double, a rebel whom he would like to have as a son. Here we have the son cut in two, divided as always into Good and Evil. Then the roles are reversed: the pseudo-evil (Henry) kills the pseudo-good (Hotspur) for the sake of the kingdom. Or, to put it another way, the King-Father finds an agent to kill the good son who has proved to be just as false as the real one; hence the brutality of this baptism of blood, the pivot of the play on which the plot balances.

> 'Be bold to tell you that I am your son,
> When I will wear a garment all of blood,
> And stain my favours in a bloody mask,
> Which washed away shall scour my shame with it . . .'

But the father's murder is no less obvious. Does not the prince kill his father's double, Falstaff, by means of a prison sentence? This, surely, is the deeper meaning of the magnificent parody in Act II, scene 4.

These scenes, heavy as wagons in a Western rumbling into the sunset, contain no lesson. The play takes us by the hand and leads us along the paths of distraction, dream or meditation. Nor do these paths diverge. It remains for you to plot your journey and for me to put on my armour and justify this preface by a confidence: this is the play which gave me my first great pleasure in the theatre. In a sense it is true to say that it decided the course of my life.

My relations with it are not really clear-headed enough for an analytical foreword, so you must press on, turn two or three pages. I wish you the same first love.

ROGER PLANCHON

Dramatis Personae

KING HENRY *the Fourth*
HENRY, *Prince of Wales*⎫
JOHN *of Lancaster*   ⎬ *sons to the King*

EARL OF WESTMORELAND
SIR WALTER BLUNT
THOMAS PERCY, *Earl of Worcester*
HENRY PERCY, *Earl of Northumberland*
HENRY PERCY, *surnamed* HOTSPUR, *his son*
EDMUND MORTIMER, *Earl of March*
RICHARD SCROOP, *Archbishop of York*
ARCHIBALD, *Earl of Douglas*
OWEN GLENDOWER
SIR RICHARD VERNON
SIR JOHN FALSTAFF
SIR MICHAEL, *a friend to the Archbishop of York*

POINS
GADSHILL
PETO
BARDOLPH
FRANCIS, *a drawer*
LADY PERCY, *wife to Hotspur, and sister to Mortimer*
LADY MORTIMER, *daughter to Glendower, and wife to Mortimer*
MISTRESS QUICKLY, *hostess of a tavern in Eastcheap*

LORDS, OFFICERS, SHERIFF, VINTNER, CHAMBERLAIN,
DRAWERS, TWO CARRIERS, TRAVELLERS, AND ATTENDANTS

SCENE: *England*

ACT FIRST

Scene One: **London. The Palace**

*Enter King Henry, Lord John of Lancaster, the Earl
of Westmoreland, Sir Walter Blunt, and others*

KING So shaken as we are, so wan with care,
Find we a time for frighted peace to pant,
And breathe short-winded accents of new broils
To be commenc'd in stronds afar remote.
No more the thirsty entrance of this soil
Shall daub her lips with her own children's blood,
No more shall trenching war channel her fields,
Nor bruise her flowerets with the armed hoofs
Of hostile paces: those opposed eyes,
Which, like the meteors of a troubled heaven,
All of one nature, of one substance bred,
Did lately meet in the intestine shock
And furious close of civil butchery,
Shall now, in mutual well-beseeming ranks,
March all one way, and be no more oppos'd
Against acquaintance, kindred and allies:
The edge of war, like an ill-sheathed knife,
No more shall cut his master: therefore, friends,
As far as to the sepulchre of Christ,
Whose soldier now, under whose blessed cross
We are impressed and engag'd to fight,
Forthwith a power of English shall we levy,
Whose arms were moulded in their mothers' womb
To chase these pagans in those holy fields,
Over whose acres walk'd those blessed feet,
Which fourteen hundred years ago were nail'd,
For our advantage, on the bitter cross.
But this our purpose now is twelve month old,
And bootless 'tis to tell you we will go:

Therefore we meet not now: then let me hear
Of you, my gentle cousin Westmoreland,
What yesternight our council did decree
In forwarding this dear expedience.

WESTMORELAND   My liege, this haste was hot in question,
And many limits of the charge set down
But yesternight, when all athwart there came
A post from Wales, loaden with heavy news,
Whose worst was that the noble Mortimer,
Leading the men of Herefordshire to fight
Against the irregular and wild Glendower,
Was by the rude hands of that Welshman taken,
A thousand of his people butchered;
Upon whose dead corpse there was such misuse,
Such beastly shameless transformation,
By those Welshwomen done, as may not be,
Without much shame, retold, or spoken of.

KING   It seems then that the tidings of this broil
Brake off our business for the Holy Land.

WESTMORELAND   This match'd with other did, my gracious lord;
For more uneven and unwelcome news
Came from the north, and thus it did import;
On Holy-rood day, the gallant Hotspur there,
Young Harry Percy, and brave Archibald,
That ever-valiant and approved Scot,
At Holmedon met,
Where they did spend a sad and bloody hour;
As by discharge of their artillery,
And shape of likelihood, the news was told;
For he that brought them, in the very heat
And pride of their contention did take horse,
Uncertain of the issue any way.

KING   Here is a dear, a true industrious friend,
Sir Walter Blunt, new lighted from his horse,
Stain'd with the variation of each soil
Betwixt that Holmedon and this seat of ours;

And he hath brought us smooth and welcome news,
The Earl of Douglas is discomfited,
Ten thousand bold Scots, two and twenty knights,
Balk'd in their own blood did Sir Walter see
On Holmedon's plains, of prisoners, Hotspur took
Mordake Earl of Fife, and eldest son
To beaten Douglas, and the Earl of Athol,
Of Murray, Angus, and Menteith:
And is not this an honourable spoil?
A gallant prize? ha, cousin, is it not?
WESTMORELAND   In faith it is.
A conquest for a prince to boast of.
KING   Yea, there thou mak'st me sad and mak'st me sin
In envy, that my Lord Northumberland
Should be the father to so blest a son:
A son who is the theme of honour's tongue,
Amongst a grove, the very straightest plant,
Who is sweet Fortune's minion and her pride,
Whilst I by looking on the praise of him
See riot and dishonour stain the brow
Of my young Harry. O that it could be prov'd
That some night-tripping fairy had exchang'd
In cradle-clothes our children where they lay,
And call'd mine Percy, his Plantagenet,
Then would I have his Harry, and he mine!
But let him from my thoughts. What think you, coz,
Of this young Percy's pride? the prisoners,
Which he in this adventure hath surpris'd,
To his own use he keeps, and sends me word
I shall have none but Mordake Earl of Fife.
WESTMORELAND   This is his uncle's teaching: this is Worcester,
Malevolent to you in all aspects,
Which makes him prune himself, and bristle up
The crest of youth against your dignity.
KING   But I have sent for him to answer this;
And for this cause awhile we must neglect

17

Our holy purpose to Jerusalem.
Cousin, on Wednesday next our council we
Will hold at Windsor; so inform the lords:
But come yourself with speed to us again,
For more is to be said and to be done
Than out of anger can be uttered.

WESTMORELAND   I will, my liege.   [*Exeunt*]

Scene Two: **London. An apartment of the Prince's**

Enter the Prince of Wales and Falstaff

FALSTAFF   Now, Hal, what time of day is it, lad?

PRINCE   Thou art so fat-witted, with drinking of old sack, and unbuttoning thee after supper, and sleeping upon benches after noon, that thou hast forgotten to demand that truly which thou wouldst truly know. What a devil hast thou to do with the time of the day? Unless hours were cups of sack, and minutes capons, and clocks the tongues of bawds, and dials the signs of leaping-houses, and the blessed sun himself a fair hot wench in flame-coloured taffeta, I see no reason why thou shouldst be so superfluous to demand the time of the day.

FALSTAFF   Indeed, you come near me now, Hal, for we that take purses go by the moon and the seven stars, and not by Phoebus, he, 'that wandering knight so fair.' And, I prithee, sweet wag, when thou art king, as, God save thy grace,— majesty I should say, for grace thou wilt have none,—

PRINCE   What, none?

FALSTAFF   No, by my troth, not so much as will serve to be prologue to an egg and butter.

PRINCE   Well, how then? come, roundly, roundly.

FALSTAFF   Marry, then, sweet wag, when thou art king, let not us that are squires of the night's body be called thieves of the day's beauty: let us be Diana's foresters, gentlemen of the shade, minions of the moon, and let men say we be men of good government, being governed as the sea is, by our noble and chaste mistress the moon, under whose countenance we steal.

PRINCE Thou sayest well, and it holds well too, for the fortune of us that are the moon's men doth ebb and flow like the sea, being governed as the sea is by the moon. As, for proof, now: a purse of gold most resolutely snatch'd on Monday night and most dissolutely spent on Tuesday morning, got with swearing 'Lay by' and spent with crying 'Bring in,' now in as low an ebb as the foot of the ladder, and by and by in as high a flow as the ridge of the gallows.

FALSTAFF By the Lord, thou say'st true, lad, and is not my hostess of the tavern a most sweet wench?

PRINCE As the honey of Hybla, my old lad of the castle, and is not a buff jerkin a most sweet robe of durance?

FALSTAFF How now, how now, mad wag? what, in thy quips and thy quiddities? what a plague have I to do with a buff jerkin?

PRINCE Why, what a pox have I to do with my hostess of the tavern?

FALSTAFF Well, thou hast call'd her to a reckoning many a a time and oft.

PRINCE Did I ever call for thee to pay thy part?

FALSTAFF No; I'll give thee thy due, thou hast paid all there.

PRINCE Yea, and elsewhere, so far as my coin would stretch, and where it would not, I have used my credit.

FALSTAFF Yea, and so us'd it that, were it not here apparent that thou art heir apparent—But, I prithee, sweet wag, shall there be gallows standing in England when thou art king? and resolution thus fobb'd as it is with the rusty curb of old father antic the law? Do not thou, when thou art king, hang a thief.

PRINCE No, thou shalt.

FALSTAFF Shall I? O rare! By the Lord, I'll be a brave judge.

PRINCE Thou judgest false already; I mean, thou shalt have the hanging of the thieves, and so become a rare hangman.

FALSTAFF Well, Hal, well, and in some sort it jumps with my humour, as well as waiting in the court, I can tell you.

PRINCE For obtaining of suits?

FALSTAFF Yea, for obtaining of suits, whereof the hangman hath no lean wardrobe. 'Sblood, I am as melancholy as a gib cat, or a lugg'd bear.

PRINCE Or an old lion, or a lover's lute.

FALSTAFF Yea, or the drone of a Lincolnshire bagpipe.

PRINCE What sayest thou to a hare, or the melancholy of Moor-ditch?

FALSTAFF Thou hast the most unsavoury similes, and art indeed the most comparative rascalliest sweet young prince. But, Hal, I prithee trouble me no more with vanity; I would to God thou and I knew where a commodity of good names were to be bought. An old lord of the council rated me the other day in the street about you, sir, but I mark'd him not, and yet he talk'd very wisely, but I regarded him not, and yet he talk'd wisely, and in the street too.

PRINCE Thou didst well, for [wisdom cries out in the streets and] no man regards it.

FALSTAFF O, thou hast damnable iteration, and art indeed able to corrupt a saint: thou hast done much harm upon me, Hal, God forgive thee for it! Before I knew thee, Hal, I knew nothing, and now am I, if a man should speak truly, little better than one of the wicked: I must give over this life, and I will give it over; by the Lord, an I do not, I am a villain; I'll be damn'd for never a king's son in Christendom.

PRINCE Where shall we take a purse to-morrow, Jack?

FALSTAFF 'Zounds, where thou wilt, lad, I'll make one; an I do not, call me villain and baffle me.

PRINCE I see a good amendment of life in thee, from praying to purse-taking.

FALSTAFF Why, Hal, 'tis my vocation, Hal, 'tis no sin for a man to labour in his vocation.

Enter Poins

Poins! Now shall we know if Gadshill have set a match. O, if men were to be sav'd by merit, what hole in hell were hot

King Henry IV

enough for him? This is the most omnipotent villain that ever
cried 'Stand' to a true man.

PRINCE Good morrow, Ned.

POINS Good morrow, sweet Hal. What say Monsieur Remorse?
what says Sir John Sack, and Sugar Jack? how agrees the devil
and thee about thy soul, that thou soldest him on Good Friday
last, for a cup of Madeira and a cold capon's leg?

PRINCE Sir John stands to his word, the devil shall have his
bargain, for he was never yet a breaker of proverbs: he will give
the devil his due.

POINS Then art thou damn'd for keeping thy word with the
devil.

PRINCE Else he had been damn'd for cozening the devil.

POINS But, my lads, my lads, to-morrow morning, by four
o'clock early at Gadshill, there are pilgrims going to Canter-
bury with rich offerings, and traders riding to London with fat
purses. I have vizards for you all, you have horses for yourselves,
Gadshill lies to-night in Rochester, I have bespoke supper
to-morrow night in Eastcheap: we may do it as secure as sleep;
if you will go, I will stuff your purses full of crowns; if you will
not, tarry at home and be hang'd.

FALSTAFF Hear ye, Yedward, if I tarry at home and go not,
I'll hang you for going.

POINS You will, chops?

FALSTAFF Hal, wilt thou make one?

PRINCE Who, I rob? I a thief? not I, by my faith.

FALSTAFF There's neither honesty, manhood, nor good fellowship in thee, nor thou cam'st not of the blood royal, if thou
darest not stand for ten shillings.

PRINCE Well then, once in my days I'll be a madcap.

FALSTAFF Why, that's well said.

PRINCE Well, come what will, I'll tarry at home.

FALSTAFF By the Lord, I'll be a traitor then, when thou art king.

PRINCE I care not.

POINS Sir John, I prithee leave the prince and me alone; I will
lay him down such reasons for this adventure that he shall go.

FALSTAFF Well, God give thee the spirit of persuasion, and him the ears of profiting, that what thou speakest, may move, and what he hears, may be believed, that the true prince may (for recreation sake) prove a false thief, for the poor abuses of the time want countenance: farewell you shall find me in Eastcheap.

PRINCE Farewell, the latter spring! farewell, All-hallown summer! *[Exit Falstaff]*

POINS Now, my good sweet honey lord, ride with us to-morrow. I have a jest to execute, that I cannot manage alone. Falstaff, Bardolph, Peto and Gadshill shall rob those men that we have already waylaid, yourself and I will not be there; and when they have the booty, if you and I do not rob them, cut this head off from my shoulders.

PRINCE How shall we part with them in setting forth?

POINS Why, we will set forth before or after them, and appoint them a place of meeting, wherein it is at our pleasure to fail; and then will they adventure upon the exploit themselves, which they shall have no sooner achiev'd but we'll set upon them.

PRINCE Yea, but 'tis like that they will know us by our horses, by our habits, and by every other appointment, to be ourselves.

POINS Tut! our horses they shall not see, I'll tie them in the wood; our vizards we will change after we leave them: and, sirrah, I have cases of buckram for the nonce, to inmask our noted outward garments.

PRINCE Yea, but I doubt they will be too hard for us.

POINS Well, for two of them, I know them to be as true-bred cowards as ever turn'd back; and for the third, if he fight longer than he sees reason, I'll forswear arms. The virtue of this jest will be the incomprehensible lies that this same fat rogue will tell us when we meet at supper, how thirty at least he fought with, what wards, what blows, what extremities he endured; and in the reproof of this lives the jest.

PRINCE Well, I'll go with thee: provide us all things necessary, and meet me to-morrow night in Eastcheap; there I'll sup. Farewell.

POINS Farewell, my lord. *[Exit]*

PRINCE I know you all, and will a while uphold
    The unyok'd humour of your idleness;
    Yet herein will I imitate the sun,
    Who doth permit the base contagious clouds
    To smother up his beauty from the world,
    That, when he please again to be himself,
    Being wanted, he may be more wonder'd at
    By breaking through the foul and ugly mists
    Of vapours that did seem to strangle him.
    If all the year were playing holidays,
    To sport would be as tedious as to work;
    But when they seldom come, they wish'd for come,
    And nothing pleaseth but rare accidents.
    So, when this loose behaviour I throw off,
    And pay the debt I never promised,
    By how much better than my word I am,
    By so much shall I falsify men's hopes,
    And like bright metal on a sullen ground,
    My reformation, glittering o'er my fault,
    Shall show more goodly, and attract more eyes,
    Than that which hath no foil to set it off.
    I'll so offend, to make offence a skill;
    Redeeming time when men think least I will.   *[Exit]*

Scene Three: **London. The Palace**

Enter the King, Northumberland, Worcester, Hotspur,
Sir Walter Blunt, with others

KING My blood hath been too cold and temperate,
    Unapt to stir at these indignities,
    And you have found me; for accordingly
    You tread upon my patience: but be sure
    I will from henceforth rather be myself,
    Mighty, and to be fear'd, than my condition,
    Which hath been smooth as oil, soft as young down,

And therefore lost that title of respect
Which the proud soul ne'er pays but to the proud.
WORCESTER Our house, my sovereign liege, little deserves
    The scourge of greatness to be us'd on it,
    And that same greatness too, which our own hands
    Have holp to make so portly.
NORTHUMBERLAND My lord,—
KING Worcester, get thee gone, for I do see
    Danger and disobedience in thine eye:
    O, sir, your presence is too bold and peremptory,
    And majesty might never yet endure
    The moody frontier of a servant brow.
    You have good leave to leave us: when we need
    Your use and counsel, we shall send for you.   [*Exit Worcester*]
    [*To Northumberland*] You were about to speak.
NORTHUMBERLAND   Yea, my good lord.
    Those prisoners in your highness' name demanded,
    Which Harry Percy here at Holmedon took,
    Were, as he says, not with such strength denied
    As is delivered to your majesty:
    Either envy, therefore, or misprision,
    Is guilty of this fault, and not my son.
HOTSPUR My liege, I did deny no prisoners;
    But I remember when the fight was done,
    When I was dry with rage, and extreme toil,
    Breathless and faint, leaning upon my sword,
    Came there a certain lord, neat and trimly dress'd,
    Fresh as a bridegroom, and his chin new reap'd
    Show'd like a stubble-land at harvest-home;
    He was perfumed like a milliner,
    And 'twixt his finger and his thumb he held
    A pouncet-box, which ever and anon
    He gave his nose, and took 't away again,
    Who therewith angry, when it next came there,
    Took it in snuff, and still he smil'd and talk'd:
    And as the soldiers bore dead bodies by,

He call'd them untaught knaves, unmannerly
To bring a slovenly unhandsome corse
Betwixt the wind and his nobility:
With many holiday and lady terms
He question'd me; amongst the rest, demanded
My prisoners in your majesty's behalf.
I then, all smarting with my wounds being cold,
To be so pester'd with a popinjay,
Out of my grief and my impatience
Answer'd neglectingly, I know not what,
He should, or he should not; for he made me mad
To see him shine so brisk, and smell so sweet,
And talk so like a waiting-gentlewoman,
Of guns, and drums, and wounds,—God save the mark!—
And telling me the sovereign'st thing on earth
Was parmaceti for an inward bruise,
And that it was great pity, so it was,
This villanous salt-petre should be digg'd
Out of the bowels of the harmless earth,
Which many a good tall fellow had destroy'd
So cowardly, and but for these vile guns
He would himself have been a soldier.
This bald unjointed chat of his, my lord,
I answer'd indirectly, as I said;
And I beseech you, let not his report
Come current for an accusation
Betwixt my love and your high majesty.
BLUNT The circumstance consider'd, good my lord,
Whate'er Lord Harry Percy then had said
To such a person, and in such a place,
At such a time, with all the rest re-told,
May reasonably die, and never rise
To do him wrong, or any way impeach
What then he said, so he unsay it now.
KING Why, yet he doth deny his prisoners,
But with proviso and exception,

That we at our own charge shall ransom straight
His brother-in-law, the foolish Mortimer,
Who, on my soul, hath wilfully betray'd
The lives of those that he did lead to fight
Against that great magician, damn'd Glendower,
Whose daughter, as we hear, the Earl of March
Hath lately married. Shall our coffers, then,
Be emptied, to redeem a traitor home?
Shall we buy treason? and indent with fears,
When they have lost and forfeited themselves?
No, on the barren mountains let him starve;
For I shall never hold that man my friend
Whose tongue shall ask me for one penny cost
To ransom home revolted Mortimer.

HOTSPUR   Revolted Mortimer!
He never did fall off, my sovereign liege,
But by the chance of war; to prove that true
Needs no more but one tongue for all those wounds,
Those mouthed wounds, which valiantly he took,
When on the gentle Severn's sedgy bank,
In single opposition, hand to hand,
He did confound the best part of an hour
In changing hardiment with great Glendower:
Three times they breath'd and three times did they drink,
Upon agreement, of swift Severn's flood,
Who then affrighted with their bloody looks
Ran fearfully among the trembling reeds,
And hid his crisp head in the hollow bank,
Bloodstained with these valiant combatants:
Never did bare and rotten policy
Colour her working with such deadly wounds,
Nor never could the noble Mortimer
Receive so many, and all willingly:
Then let not him be slander'd with revolt.

KING   Thou dost belie him, Percy, thou dost belie him;
He never did encounter with Glendower:

26

I tell thee,
He durst as well have met the devil alone
As Owen Glendower for an enemy.
Art thou not asham'd? But, sirrah, henceforth
Let me not hear you speak of Mortimer:
Send me your prisoners with the speediest means,
Or you shall hear in such a kind from me
As will displease you. My lord Northumberland,
We license your departure with your son;
Send us your prisoners, or you will hear of it.

                    [Exeunt King Henry, Blunt, and train]

HOTSPUR   An if the devil come and roar for them,
  I will not send them: I will after straight
  And tell him so, for I will ease my heart,
  Albeit I make a hazard of my head.
NORTHUMBERLAND   What, drunk with choler? stay, and
    pause a while:
  Here comes your uncle.

Re-enter Worcester

HOTSPUR   Speak of Mortimer?
  'Zounds, I will speak of him, and let my soul
  Want mercy, if I do not join with him:
  Yea, on his part I'll empty all these veins,
  And shed my dear blood, drop by drop in the dust,
  But I will lift the down-trod Mortimer
  As high in the air as this unthankful king,
  As this ingrate and canker'd Bolingbroke.
NORTHUMBERLAND   Brother, the king hath made your
    nephew mad.
WORCESTER   Who struck this heat up after I was gone?
HOTSPUR   He will, forsooth, have all my prisoners,
  And when I urg'd the ransom once again
  Of my wife's brother, then his cheek look'd pale,
  And on my face he turn'd an eye of death,
  Trembling even at the name of Mortimer.

WORCESTER   I cannot blame him, was not he proclaim'd
 By Richard that dead is the next of blood?
NORTHUMBERLAND   He was, I heard the proclamation:
 And then it was when the unhappy king
 (Whose wrongs in us God pardon!) did set forth
 Upon his Irish expedition;
 From whence he intercepted did return
 To be depos'd, and shortly murdered.
WORCESTER   And for whose death we in the world's wide mouth
 Live scandaliz'd and foully spoken of.
HOTSPUR   But soft, I pray you, did King Richard then
 Proclaim my brother Edmund Mortimer
 Heir to the crown?
NORTHUMBERLAND   He did, myself did hear it.
HOTSPUR   Nay then I cannot blame his cousin king,
 That wish'd him on the barren mountains starve;
 But shall it be that you, that set the crown
 Upon the head of this forgetful man,
 And for his sake wear the detested blot
 Of murderous subornation, shall it be
 That you a world of curses undergo,
 Being the agents, or base second means,
 The cords, the ladder, or the hangman rather—
 O pardon me, that I descend so low,
 To show the line and the predicament,
 Wherein you range under this subtle king—
 Shall it for shame be spoken in these days,
 Or fill up chronicles in time to come,
 That men of your nobility and power
 Did gage them both in an unjust behalf,
 (As both of you, God pardon it, have done)
 To put down Richard, that sweet lovely rose,
 And plant this thorn, this canker, Bolingbroke?
 And shall it in more shame be further spoken,
 That you are fool'd, discarded, and shook off
 By him, for whom these shames ye underwent?

28

No, yet time serves, wherein you may redeem
Your banish'd honours, and restore yourselves
Into the good thoughts of the world again:
Revenge the jeering and disdain'd contempt
Of this proud king, who studies day and night
To answer all the debt he owes to you
Even with the bloody payment of your deaths:
Therefore, I say,—

WORCESTER   Peace, cousin, say no more:
And now I will unclasp a secret book,
And to your quick-conceiving discontents
I'll read you matter deep and dangerous,
As full of peril and adventurous spirit
As to o'er-walk a current roaring loud,
On the unsteadfast footing of a spear.

HOTSPUR   If he fall in, good night, or sink, or swim:
Send danger from the east unto the west,
So honour cross it, from the north to south,
And let them grapple: O, the blood more stirs
To rouse a lion than to start a hare!

NORTHUMBERLAND   Imagination of some great exploit
Drives him beyond the bounds of patience.

HOTSPUR   By heaven, methinks it were an easy leap,
To pluck bright honour from the pale-fac'd moon,
Or dive into the bottom of the deep,
Where fathom-line could never touch the ground,
And pluck up drowned honour by the locks,
So he that doth redeem her thence might wear
Without corrival all her dignities,
But out upon this half-fac'd fellowship!

WORCESTER   He apprehends a world of figures here,
But not the form of what he should attend;
Good cousin, give me audience for a while.

HOTSPUR   I cry you mercy.

WORCESTER   Those same noble Scots
That are your prisoners,—

HOTSPUR   I'll keep them all;
  By God, he shall not have a Scot of them,
  No, if a Scot would save his soul, he shall not:
  I'll keep them by this hand.
WORCESTER   You start away,
  And lend no ear unto my purposes:
  Those prisoners you shall keep.
HOTSPUR   Nay, I will; that's flat:
  He said he would not ransom Mortimer,
  Forbad my tongue to speak of Mortimer,
  But I will find him when he lies asleep,
  And in his ear I'll holla 'Mortimer!'
  Nay,
  I'll have a starling shall be taught to speak
  Nothing but 'Mortimer,' and give it him,
  To keep his anger still in motion.
WORCESTER   Hear you, cousin, a word.
HOTSPUR   All studies here I solemnly defy,
  Save how to gall and pinch this Bolingbroke,
  And that same sword-and-buckler Prince of Wales,
  But that I think his father loves him not,
  And would be glad he met with some mischance,
  I would have him poison'd with a pot of ale.
WORCESTER   Farewell, kinsman; I'll talk to you
  When you are better temper'd to attend.
NORTHUMBERLAND   Why, what a wasp-stung and impatient
    fool
  Art thou to break into this woman's mood,
  Tying thine ear to no tongue but thine own!
HOTSPUR   Why, look you, I am whipp'd and scourg'd with
    rods,
  Nettled, and stung with pismires, when I hear
  Of this vile politician, Bolingbroke,
  In Richard's time,—what do you call the place?—
  A plague upon it, it is in Gloucestershire;
  'Twas where the madcap duke his uncle kept,

His uncle York, where I first bow'd my knee
Unto this king of smiles, this Bolingbroke,—
'Sblood!—
When you and he came back from Ravenspurgh.
NORTHUMBERLAND   At Berkley-castle.
HOTSPUR   You say true:
Why, what a candy deal of courtesy
This fawning greyhound then did proffer me,
Look, 'when his infant fortune came to age,'
And 'gentle Harry Percy,' and 'kind cousin;'
O, the devil take such cozeners! God forgive me!
Good uncle, tell your tale, I have done.
WORCESTER   Nay, if you have not, to it again;
We will stay your leisure.
HOTSPUR   I have done, i' faith.
WORCESTER   Then once more to your Scottish prisoners;
Deliver them up without their ransom straight,
And make the Douglas' son your only mean
For powers in Scotland, which, for divers reasons
Which I shall send you written, be assur'd,
Will easily be granted. You, my lord,   [To Northumberland]
Your son in Scotland being thus employ'd,
Shall secretly into the bosom creep
Of that same noble prelate well belov'd,
The archbishop.
HOTSPUR   Of York, is it not?
WORCESTER   True; who bears hard
His brother's death at Bristowe, the Lord Scroop.
I speak not this in estimation,
As what I think might be, but what I know
Is ruminated, plotted, and set down,
And only stays but to behold the face
Of that occasion that shall bring it on.
HOTSPUR   I smell it. Upon my life, it will do well.
NORTHUMBERLAND   Before the game is a-foot thou still let'st
   slip.

HOTSPUR   Why, it cannot choose but be a noble plot,
And then the power of Scotland, and of York,
To join with Mortimer, ha?
WORCESTER   And so they shall.
HOTSPUR   In faith, it is exceedingly well aim'd.
WORCESTER   And 'tis no little reason bids us speed,
To save our heads by raising of a head:
For, bear ourselves as even as we can,
The king will always think him in our debt,
And think we think ourselves unsatisfied,
Till he hath found a time to pay us home:
And see already how he doth begin
To make us strangers to his looks of love.
HOTSPUR   He does, he does: we'll be reveng'd on him.
WORCESTER   Cousin, farewell. No further go in this
Than I by letters shall direct your course.
When time is ripe, which will be suddenly,
I'll steal to Glendower and Lord Mortimer,
Where you and Douglas and our powers at once,
As I will fashion it, shall happily meet,
To bear our fortunes in our own strong arms,
Which now we hold at much uncertainty.
NORTHUMBERLAND   Farewell, good brother; we shall thrive,
I trust.
HOTSPUR   Uncle, adieu: O, let the hours be short
Till fields, and blows, and groans, applaud our sport! [*Exeunt*]

ACT SECOND

Scene One: **Rochester. An Inn Yard**

Enter a Carrier with a lantern in his hand

FIRST CARRIER Heigh-ho! an it be not four by the day, I'll be hang'd: Charles' wain is over the new chimney, and yet our horse not pack'd. What, ostler!

OSTLER (*within*) Anon, anon.

FIRST CARRIER I prithee, Tom, beat Cut's saddle, put a few flocks in the point; poor jade is wrung in the withers, out of all cess.

Enter another Carrier

SECOND CARRIER Peas and beans are as dank here as a dog, and that is the next way to give poor jades the bots: this house is turn'd upside down since Robin Ostler died.

FIRST CARRIER Poor fellow never joyed since the price of oats rose, it was the death of him.

SECOND CARRIER I think this be the most villanous house in all London road for fleas, I am stung like a tench.

FIRST CARRIER Like a tench? by the mass, there is ne'er a king christen could be better bit than I have been since the first cock.

SECOND CARRIER Why, they will allow us ne'er a jordan, and then we leak in your chimney, and your chamber-lie breeds fleas like a loach.

FIRST CARRIER What, ostler! come away and be hang'd! come away.

SECOND CARRIER I have a gammon of bacon, and two razes of ginger, to be delivered as far as Charing-cross.

FIRST CARRIER God's body, the turkeys in my pannier are quite starv'd. What, ostler! A plague on thee, hast thou never any eye in thy head? canst not hear? An 'twere not as good deed

33

as drink, to break the pate on thee, I am a very villain. Come
and be hang'd! hast no faith in thee?

Enter Gadshill

GADSHILL   Good morrow, carriers; what's o'clock?

FIRST CARRIER   I think it be two o'clock.

GADSHILL   I prithee, lend me thy lantern, to see my gelding in
the stable.

FIRST CARRIER   Nay, by God, soft, I know a trick worth two
of that, i' faith.

GADSHILL   I pray thee, lend me thine.

SECOND CARRIER   Ay, when? canst tell? Lend me thy lantern,
quoth he? marry, I'll see thee hang'd first.

GADSHILL Sirrah carrier, what time do you mean to come to
London?

SECOND CARRIER   Time enough to go to bed with a candle, I
warrant thee. Come, neighbour Mugs, we'll call up the
gentlemen: they will along with company, for they have great
charge.   [*Exeunt Carriers*]

GADSHILL   What ho! chamberlain!

CHAMBERLAIN (*within*)   At hand, quoth pick-purse.

GADSHILL   That's even as fair as—at hand, quoth the chamberlain; for thou variest no more from picking of purses than
giving direction doth from labouring; thou layest the plot how.

Enter Chamberlain

CHAMBERLAIN   Good morrow, Master Gadshill. It holds
current that I told you yesternight, there's a franklin in the
weald of Kent hath brought three hundred marks with him in
gold; I heard him tell it to one of his company last night at
supper, a kind of auditor, one that hath abundance of charge
too, God knows what; they are up already, and call for eggs
and butter; they will away presently.

GADSHILL   Sirrah, if they meet not with Saint Nicholas' clerks,
I'll give thee this neck.

CHAMBERLAIN   No, I'll none of it: I pray thee keep that for
the hangman, for I know thou worshippest Saint Nicholas, as
truly as a man of falsehood may.

GADSHILL   What talkest thou to me of the hangman? if I hang,
I'll make a fat pair of gallows: for if I hang, old Sir John hangs
with me, and thou knowest he is no starveling. Tut! there are
other Trojans that thou dream'st not of, the which for sport
sake are content to do the profession some grace, that would, if
matters should be look'd into, for their own credit sake make all
whole. I am join'd with no foot landrakers, no long-staff
sixpenny strikers, none of these mad mustachio purple-hued
malt-worms, but with nobility and tranquillity, burgomasters
and great oneyers, such as can hold in, such as will strike sooner
than speak, and speak sooner than drink, and drink sooner
than pray, and yet, 'zounds, I lie, for they pray continually to
their saint, the commonwealth, or rather, not pray to her, but
prey on her, for they ride up and down on her, and make her
their boots.

CHAMBERLAIN   What, the commonwealth their boots? will she
hold out water in foul way?

GADSHILL   She will, she will, justice hath liquor'd her. We steal
as in a castle, cock-sure; we have the receipt of fern-seed, we
walk invisible.

CHAMBERLAIN   Nay, by my faith, I think you are more
beholding to the night than to fern-seed for your walking
invisible.

GADSHILL   Give me thy hand, thou shalt have a share in our
purchase, as I am a true man.

CHAMBERLAIN   Nay, rather let me have it, as you are a false
thief.

GADSHILL   Go to; 'homo' is a common name to all men: bid
the osler bring my gelding out of the stable; farewell, you
muddy knave.   [*Exeunt*]

Scene Two: **The Highway, near Gadshill**

Enter Prince Henry and Poins

POINS Come, shelter, shelter; I have remov'd Falstaff's horse, and he frets like a gumm'd velvet.
PRINCE Stand close.

Enter Falstaff

FALSTAFF Poins, Poins, and be hanged, Poins!
PRINCE Peace, ye fat-kidney'd rascal, what a brawling dost thou keep?
FALSTAFF Where's Poins, Hal?
PRINCE He is walk'd up to the top of the hill; I'll go seek him.
FALSTAFF I am accurs'd to rob in that thief's company: the rascal hath removed my horse, and tied him I know not where; if I travel but four foot by the squire further afoot, I shall break my wind. Well, I doubt not but to die a fair death for all this, if I 'scape hanging for killing that rogue. I have forsworn his company hourly any time this two and twenty years, and yet I am bewitch'd with the rogue's company. If the rascal have not given me medicines to make me love him, I'll be hang'd. It could not be else; I have drunk medicines. Poins! Hal! a plague upon you both! Bardolph! Peto! I'll starve ere I'll rob a foot further. An 'twere not as good a deed as drink to turn true man, and to leave these rogues, I am the veriest varlet that ever chewed with a tooth. Eight yards of uneven ground is threescore and ten miles afoot with me, and the stony-hearted villains know it well enough, a plague upon it when thieves cannot be true one to another! (*They whistle.*) Whew! A plague upon you all, give me my horse, you rogues, give me my horse, and be hang'd!
PRINCE Peace, ye fat-guts! lie down, lay thine ear close to the ground, and list if thou canst hear the tread of travellers.
FALSTAFF Have you any levers to lift me up again being down? 'Sblood, I'll not bear mine own flesh so far afoot again for all

Falstaff

the coin in thy father's exchequer. What a plague mean ye to colt me thus?

PRINCE   Thou liest; thou art not colted, thou art uncolted.

FALSTAFF   I prithee, good prince, Hal, help me to my horse, good king's son.

PRINCE   Out, ye rogue! shall I be your ostler?

FALSTAFF   Go hang thyself in thine own heir-apparent garters! If I be ta'en, I'll peach for this. An I have not ballads made on you all, and sung to filthy tunes, let a cup of sack be my poison: when a jest is so forward, and afoot too! I hate it.

Enter Gadshill, Bardolph and Peto with him

GADSHILL   Stand.

FALSTAFF   So I do, against my will.

POINS   O, 'tis our setter, I know his voice. Bardolph, what news?

BARDOLPH   Case ye, case ye, on with your vizards; there's money of the king's coming down the hill, 'tis going to the king's exchequer.

FALSTAFF   You lie, ye rogue; 'tis going to the king's tavern.

GADSHILL   There's enough to make us all.

FALSTAFF   To be hang'd.

PRINCE   Sirs,
You four shall front them in the narrow lane;
Ned Poins and I will walk lower; if they 'scape
From your encounter, then they light on us.

PETO   How many be there of them?

GADSHILL   Some eight or ten.

FALSTAFF   'Zounds, will they not rob us?

PRINCE   What, a coward, Sir John Paunch?

FALSTAFF   Indeed, I am not John of Gaunt, your grandfather, but yet no coward, Hal.

PRINCE   Well, we leave that to the proof.

POINS   Sirrah Jack, thy horse stands behind the hedge; when thou need'st him, there thou shalt find him: farewell, and stand fast.

FALSTAFF   Now cannot I strike him, if I should be hang'd.

PRINCE Ned, where are our disguises?

POINS Here, hard by, stand close. [*Exeunt Prince and Poins*]

FALSTAFF Now, my masters, happy man be his dole, say I: every man to his business.

Enter the Travellers

FIRST TRAVELLER Come, neighbour, the boy shall lead our horses down the hill, we'll walk afoot awhile, and ease our legs.

THIEVES Stand!

TRAVELLERS Jesus bless us!

FALSTAFF Strike, down with them, cut the villains' throats: ah! whoreson caterpillars, bacon-fed knaves! they hate us youth, down with them, fleece them.

TRAVELLERS O, we are undone, both we and ours for ever!

FALSTAFF Hang ye, gorbellied knaves, are ye undone? No, ye fat chuffs, I would your store were here! On, bacons, on! What, ye knaves? young men must live; you are grandjurors, are ye? we'll jure ye, 'faith. [*Here they rob them and bind them. Exeunt*]

Re-enter Prince Henry and Poins disguised

PRINCE The thieves have bound the true men; now could thou and I rob the thieves, and go merrily to London, it would be argument for a week, laughter for a month, and a good jest for ever.

POINS Stand close, I hear them coming.

Enter the Thieves again

FALSTAFF Come, my masters, let us share, and then to horse before day; an the Prince and Poins be not two arrant cowards, there's no equity stirring: there's no more valour in that Poins than in a wild-duck.

PRINCE Your money!

POINS Villains!

As they are sharing, the Prince and Poins set upon them; they all run away; and Falstaff, after a blow or two, runs away too, leaving the booty behind them

PRINCE   Got with much ease. Now merrily to horse:
  The thieves are all scatter'd and possess'd with fear
  So strongly that they dare not meet each other;
  Each takes his fellow for an officer.
  Away, good Ned. Falstaff sweats to death,
  And lards the lean earth as he walks along:
  Were't not for laughing, I should pity him.
POINS   How the rogue roar'd!   [*Exeunt*]

Scene Three: **Warkworth Castle**

Enter Hotspur solus, reading a letter

HOTSPUR   'But, for mine own part, my lord, I could be well
contented to be there, in respect of the love I bear your house.'
He could be contented: why is he not, then? In respect of the
love he bears our house: he shows in this, he loves his
own barn better than he loves our house. Let me see
some more. 'The purpose you undertake is dangerous;'—
why, that's certain: 'tis dangerous to take a cold, to sleep, to
drink; but I tell you, my lord fool, out of this nettle danger, we
pluck this flower safety. 'The purpose you undertake is dangerous, the friends you have named uncertain, the time itself
unsorted, and your whole plot too light, for the counterpoise of
so great an opposition.' Say you so, say you so, I say unto you
again, you are a shallow cowardly hind, and you lie. What a
lack-brain is this! By the Lord, our plot is a good plot as ever
was laid, our friends true and constant: a good plot, good
friends, and full of expectation; an excellent plot, very good
friends. What a frosty-spirited rogue is this! Why, my lord of
York commends the plot, and the general course of the action.
'Zounds, an I were now by this rascal, I could brain him with
his lady's fan. Is there not my father, my uncle, and myself; lord
Edmund Mortimer, my lord of York, and Owen Glendower; is
there not besides the Douglas, have I not all their letters to
meet me in arms by the ninth of the next month, and are they

not some of them set forward already? What a pagan rascal is
this, an infidel! Ha! you shall see now in very sincerity of fear
and cold heart, will he to the king, and lay open all our proceedings. O, I could divide myself, and go to buffets, for moving
such a dish of skim milk with so honourable an action! Hang
him! let him tell the king: we are prepared. I will set forward
to-night.

Enter Lady Percy

How now, Kate! I must leave you within these two hours.
LADY PERCY   O, my good lord, why are you thus alone?
For what offence have I this fortnight been
A banish'd woman from my Harry's bed?
Tell me, sweet lord, what is 't that takes from thee
Thy stomach, pleasure, and thy golden sleep?
Why dost thou bend thine eyes upon the earth?
And start so often when thou sit'st alone?
Why hast thou lost the fresh blood in thy cheeks?
And given my treasures and my rights of thee
To thick-ey'd musing, and curs'd melancholy?
In thy faint slumbers I by thee have watch'd,
And heard thee murmur tales of iron wars,
Speak terms of manage to thy bounding steed,
Cry 'Courage! to the field!' And thou hast talk'd
Of sallies and retires, of trenches, tents,
Of palisadoes, frontiers, parapets,
Of basilisks, of cannon, culverin,
Of prisoners' ransom, and of soldiers slain,
And all the currents of a heady fight;
Thy spirit within thee hath been so at war,
And thus hath so bestirr'd thee in thy sleep,
That beads of sweat have stood upon thy brow,
Like bubbles in a late-disturbed stream,
And in thy face strange motions have appear'd,
Such as we see when men restrain their breath,
On some great sudden hest. O, what portents are these?

Some heavy business hath my lord in hand,
And I must know it, else he loves me not.
HOTSPUR   What ho!

Enter Servant

               Is Gilliams with the packet gone?
SERVANT   He is, my lord, an hour ago.
HOTSPUR   Hath Butler brought those horses from the sheriff?
SERVANT   One horse, my lord, he brought even now.
HOTSPUR   What horse? Roan, a crop-ear, is it not?
SERVANT   It is, my lord.
HOTSPUR   That roan shall be my throne.
  Well, I will back him straight: O esperance!
  Bid Butler lead him forth into the park.   [*Exit Servant*]
LADY PERCY   But hear you, my lord.
HOTSPUR   What say'st thou, my lady?
LADY PERCY   What is it carries you away?
HOTSPUR   Why, my horse, my love, my horse.
LADY PERCY   Out, you mad-headed ape!
  A weasel hath not such a deal of spleen
  As you are toss'd with. In faith,
  I'll know your business, Harry, that I will.
  I fear my brother Mortimer doth stir
  About his title, and hath sent for you
  To line his enterprize: but if you go—
HOTSPUR   So far afoot, I shall be weary, love.
LADY PERCY   Come, come, you paraquito, answer me
  Directly unto this question that I ask:
  In faith, I'll break thy little finger, Harry,
  An if thou wilt not tell me all things true.
HOTSPUR   Away,
  Away, you trifler! Love, I love thee not,
  I care not for thee, Kate, this is no world
  To play with mammets and to tilt with lips,
  We must have bloody noses, and crack'd crowns,

And pass them current too. God's me, my horse!
What say'st thou, Kate? what wouldst thou have with me?
LADY PERCY   Do you not love me? do you not, indeed?
Well, do not then, for since you love me not,
I will not love myself. Do you not love me?
Nay, tell me if you speak in jest or no.
HOTSPUR   Come, wilt thou see me ride?
And when I am a horseback, I will swear
I love thee infinitely. But hark you, Kate;
I must not have you henceforth question me
Whither I go, nor reason whereabout:
Whither I must, I must, and, to conclude,
This evening must I leave you, gentle Kate.
I know you wise, but yet no farther wise
Than Harry Percy's wife: constant you are,
But yet a woman: and for secrecy,
No lady closer, for I well believe
Thou wilt not utter what thou dost not know;
And so far will I trust thee, gentle Kate.
LADY PERCY   How? so far?
HOTSPUR   Not an inch further; but hark you, Kate:
Whither I go, thither shall you go too;
To-day will I set forth, to-morrow you.
Will this content you, Kate?
LADY PERCY   It must of force.   [*Exeunt*]

Scene Four: **The Boar's-Head Tavern in Eastcheap**

Enter the Prince, and Poins

PRINCE   Ned, prithee come out of that fat room, and lend me
thy hand to laugh a little.
POINS   Where hast been, Hal?
PRINCE   With three or four loggerheads, amongst three or four-
score hogsheads. I have sounded the very base-string of humility.

Sirrah, I am sworn brother to a leash of drawers, and can call them all by their christen names, as Tom, Dick, and Francis. They take it already upon their salvation, that though I be but Prince of Wales, yet I am the king of courtesy, and tell me flatly I am no proud Jack, like Falstaff, but a Corinthian, a lad of mettle, a good boy (by the Lord, so they call me) and when I am king of England, I shall command all the good lads in Eastcheap. They call drinking deep, dyeing scarlet, and when you breathe in your watering, they cry 'hem!' and bid you play it off. To conclude, I am so good a proficient in one quarter of an hour, that I can drink with any tinker in his own language during my life. I tell thee, Ned, thou hast lost much honour, that thou wert not with me in this action. But, sweet Ned,—to sweeten which name of Ned, I give thee this pennyworth of sugar, clapp'd even now into my hand by an underskinker, one that never spake other English in his life than 'Eight shillings and sixpence,' and 'You are welcome,' with this shrill addition, 'Anon, anon, sir! Score a pint of bastard in the Half-moon,' or so. But, Ned, to drive away the time till Falstaff come, I prithee, do thou stand in some by-room, while I question my puny drawer to what end he gave me the sugar, and do thou never leave calling 'Francis,' that his tale to me may be nothing but 'Anon.' Step aside, and I'll show thee a precedent.

POINS   Francis!
PRINCE   Thou art perfect.
POINS   Francis!   [*Exit Poins*]

Enter Francis

FRANCIS   Anon, anon, sir. Look down into the Pomgarnet, Ralph.
PRINCE   Come hither, Francis.
FRANCIS   My lord?
PRINCE   How long hast thou to serve, Francis?
FRANCIS   Forsooth, five years, and as much as to—
POINS (*within*)   Francis!
FRANCIS   Anon, anon, sir.

PRINCE Five year! by'r lady, a long lease for the clinking of pewter. But, Francis, darest thou be so valiant as to play the coward with thy indenture, and show it a fair pair of heels, and run from it?

FRANCIS O Lord, sir, I'll be sworn upon all the books in England, I could find in my heart.

POINS (*within*) Francis!

FRANCIS Anon, sir.

PRINCE How old art thou, Francis?

FRANCIS Let me see—about Michaelmas next I shall be—

POINS (*within*) Francis!

FRANCIS Anon, sir, pray stay a little, my lord.

PRINCE Nay, but hark you, Francis: for the sugar thou gavest me, 'twas a pennyworth, was 't not?

FRANCIS O Lord, I would it had been two!

PRINCE I will give thee for it a thousand pound: ask me when thou wilt, and thou shalt have it.

POINS (*within*) Francis!

FRANCIS Anon, anon.

PRINCE Anon, Francis? No, Francis; but to-morrow, Francis; or Francis, o' Thursday; or indeed, Francis, when thou wilt. But, Francis!

FRANCIS My lord?

PRINCE Wilt thou rob this leathern jerkin, crystal-button, not-pated, agate-ring, puke-stocking, caddis-garter, smooth-tongue, Spanish pouch?

FRANCIS O lord, sir, who do you mean?

PRINCE Why, then, your brown bastard is your only drink; for look you, Francis, your white canvas doublet will sully; in Barbary, sir, it cannot come to so much.

FRANCIS What, sir?

POINS (*within*) Francis!

PRINCE Away, you rogue! dost thou not hear them call?

Here they both call him; the drawer stands amazed, not knowing which way to go

44

Enter Vintner

VINTNER   What, stand'st thou still, and hear'st such a calling?
Look to the guests within. (*Exit Francis.*) My lord, old Sir John
with half-a-dozen more are at the door: shall I let them in?
PRINCE   Let them alone awhile, and then open the door. (*Exit
Vintner.*) Poins!

Re-enter Poins

POINS   Anon, anon, sir.
PRINCE   Sirrah, Falstaff and the rest of the thieves are at the
door: shall we be merry?
POINS   As merry as crickets, my lad. But hark ye, what cunning
match have you made with this jest of the drawer? come, what's
the issue?
PRINCE   I am now of all humours, that have showed themselves
humours since the old days of goodman Adam to the pupil age
of this present twelve o'clock at midnight.
What's o'clock, Francis?
FRANCIS   Anon, anon, sir.
PRINCE   That ever this fellow should have fewer words than a
parrot, and yet the son of a woman! His industry is up-stairs
and down-stairs, his eloquence the parcel of a reckoning. I am
not yet of Percy's mind, the Hotspur of the north, he that kills
me some six or seven dozen of Scots at a breakfast; washes his
hands, and says to his wife 'Fie upon this quiet life! I want
work.' 'O my sweet Harry,' says she, 'how many hast thou
kill'd to-day?' 'Give my roan horse a drench,' says he; and
answers 'some fourteen,' an hour after; 'a trifle, a trifle,' I
prithee, call in Falstaff: I'll play Percy, and that damn'd
brawn shall play Dame Mortimer his wife. 'Rivo!' says the
drunkard. Call in ribs, call in tallow.

*Enter Falstaff, Gadshill, Bardolph, and Peto ;
Francis following with wine*

POINS   Welcome, Jack: where hast thou been?

FALSTAFF A plague of all cowards, I say, and a vengeance too, marry and amen! Give me a cup of sack, boy. Ere I lead this life long, I'll sew nether stocks and mend them and foot them too. A plague of all cowards! Give me a cup of sack, rogue. Is there no virtue extant? [*He drinks*]

PRINCE Didst thou never see Titan kiss a dish of butter? pitiful-hearted butter, that melted at the sweet tale of the sun's! if thou didst, then behold that compound.

FALSTAFF You rogue, here's lime in this sack too: there is nothing but roguery to be found in villanous man: yet a coward is worse than a cup of sack with lime in it. A villanous coward! Go thy ways, old Jack, die when thou wilt, if manhood, good manhood, be not forgot upon the face of the earth, then am I a shotten herring. There lives not three good men unhang'd in England, and one of them is fat, and grows old, God help the while! a bad world, I say, I would I were a weaver; I could sing psalms or any thing. A plague of all cowards, I say still.

PRINCE How now, wool-sack, what mutter you?

FALSTAFF A king's son! If I do not beat thee out of thy kingdom with a dagger of lath, and drive all thy subjects afore thee like a flock of wild-geese, I'll never wear hair on my face more, you Prince of Wales!

PRINCE Why, you whoreson round man, what's the matter?

FALSTAFF Are not you a coward? answer me to that, and Poins there?

POINS 'Zounds, ye fat paunch, an ye call me coward, by the Lord, I'll stab thee.

FALSTAFF I call thee coward? I'll see thee damn'd ere I call thee coward, but I would give a thousand pound I could run as fast as thou canst. You are straight enough in the shoulders, you care not who sees your back: call you that backing of your friends? A plague upon such backing! give me them that will face me, give me a cup of sack: I am a rogue, if I drunk to-day.

PRINCE O villain! thy lips are scarce wip'd since thou drunk'st last.

FALSTAFF All is one for that. (*He drinks.*) A plague of all cowards,
still say I.

PRINCE What's the matter?

FALSTAFF What's the matter? there be four of us here have
ta'en a thousand pound this day morning.

PRINCE Where is it, Jack, where is it?

FALSTAFF Where is it? taken from us it is: a hundred upon poor
four of us.

PRINCE What, a hundred, man?

FALSTAFF I am a rogue, if I were not at half-sword with a
dozen of them two hours together. I have 'scap'd by miracle.
I am eight times thrust through the doublet, four through the
hose, my buckler cut through and through, my sword hack'd
like a handsaw—*ecce signum*! I never dealt better since I was a
man: all would not do. A plague of all cowards! Let them
speak: if they speak more or less than truth, they are villains,
and the sons of darkness.

PRINCE Speak, sirs, how was it?

GADSHILL We four set upon some dozen—

FALSTAFF Sixteen at least, my lord.

GADSHILL And bound them.

PETO No, no, they were not bound.

FALSTAFF You rogue, they were bound, every man of them, or
I am a Jew else; an Ebrew Jew.

GADSHILL As we were sharing, some six or seven fresh men set
upon us—

FALSTAFF And unbound the rest, and then come in the other.

PRINCE What, fought you with them all?

FALSTAFF All? I know not what you call all; but if I fought
not with fifty of them, I am a bunch of radish: if there were
not two or three and fifty upon poor old Jack, then am I no
two-legg'd creature.

PRINCE Pray God you have not murder'd some of them.

FALSTAFF Nay, that's past praying for: I have pepper'd two of
them; two I am sure I have paid, two rogues in buckram suits.
I tell thee what, Hal, if I tell thee a lie, spit in my face, call me

47

horse; thou knowest my old ward; here I lay, and thus I bore
my point, four rogues in buckram let drive at me—

PRINCE   What, four? thou saidst but two even now.

FALSTAFF   Four, Hal, I told thee four.

POINS   Ay, ay, he said four.

FALSTAFF   These four came all a-front, and mainly thrust at
me, I made me no more ado, but took all their seven points in
my target, thus.

PRINCE   Seven? why, there were but four even now.

FALSTAFF   In buckram?

POINS   Ay, four, in buckram suits.

FALSTAFF   Seven, by these hilts, or I am a villain else.

PRINCE   Prithee let him alone, we shall have more anon.

FALSTAFF   Dost thou hear me, Hal?

PRINCE   Ay, and mark thee too, Jack.

FALSTAFF   Do so, for it is worth the listening to; these nine in
buckram that I told thee of,—

PRINCE   So, two more already.

FALSTAFF   Their points being broken,—

POINS   Down fell their hose.

FALSTAFF   Began to give me ground: but I followed me close,
came in foot and hand, and with a thought seven of the eleven
I paid.

PRINCE   O monstrous! eleven buckram men grown out of two!

FALSTAFF   But, as the devil would have it, three misbegotten
knaves in Kendal green came at my back, and let drive at me,
for it was so dark, Hal, that thou couldst not see thy hand.

PRINCE   These lies are like their father that begets them,
Gross as a mountain, open, palpable.
Why, thou clay-brain'd guts, thou knotty-pated fool,
Thou whoreson obscene greasy tallow-catch,—

FALSTAFF   What, art thou mad? art thou mad? is not the truth
the truth?

PRINCE   Why, how couldst thou know these men in Kendal
green, when it was so dark thou couldst not see thy hand?
come, tell us your reason. What sayest thou to this?

POINS Come, your reason, Jack, your reason.

FALSTAFF What, upon compulsion? 'Zounds, an I were at the strappado, or all the racks in the world, I would not tell you on compulsion. Give you a reason on compulsion? if reasons were as plentiful as blackberries, I would give no man a reason upon compulsion, I.

PRINCE I'll be no longer guilty of this sin;
This sanguine coward, this bed-presser,
This horseback-breaker, this huge hill of flesh,—

FALSTAFF 'Sblood, you starveling, you elf-skin, you dried neat's tongue, you bull's pizzle, you stock-fish! O for breath to utter what is like thee, you tailor's-yard, you sheath, you bow-case, you vile standing-tuck,—

PRINCE Well, breathe a while, and then to it again, and when thou hast tired thyself in base comparisons, hear me speak but this.

POINS Mark, Jack.

PRINCE We two saw you four set on four and bound them, and were masters of their wealth. Mark now how a plain tale shall put you down; then did we two set on you four, and, with a word, out-fac'd you from your prize, and have it, yea, and can show it you here in the house: and, Falstaff, you carried your guts away as nimbly, with as quick dexerity, and roar'd for mercy, and still run and roar'd, as ever I heard bull-calf. What a slave art thou, to hack thy sword as thou hast done; and then say it was in fight! What trick, what device, what starting-hole, canst thou now find out, to hide thee from this open and apparent shame?

POINS Come, let's hear, Jack, what trick hast thou now?

FALSTAFF By the Lord, I knew ye as well as he that made ye. Why, hear you, my masters, was it for me to kill the heir-apparent? should I turn upon the true prince? why, thou knowest I am as valiant as Hercules: but beware instinct, the lion will not touch the true prince, instinct is a great matter; I was now a coward on instinct. I shall think the better of myself and thee during my life; I for a valiant lion, and thou for a true

49

prince. But, by the Lords, lads, I am glad you have the money; hostess, clap to the doors, watch to-night, pray to-morrow, gallants, lads, boys, hearts of gold, all the titles of good fellowship come to you! What, shall we be merry? shall we have a play extempore?

PRINCE   Content, and the argument shall be thy running away.

FALSTAFF   Ah, no more of that, Hal, an thou lovest me!

Enter Mistress Quickly

MISTRESS QUICKLY   Jesu, my lord the prince!

PRINCE   How now, my lady the hostess, what say'st thou to me?

MISTRESS QUICKLY   Marry, my lord, there is a nobleman of the court at door would speak with you: he says he comes from your father.

PRINCE   Give him as much as will make him a royal man, and send him back again to my mother.

FALSTAFF   What manner of man is he?

MISTRESS QUICKLY   An old man.

FALSTAFF   What doth gravity out of his bed at midnight? Shall I give him his answer?

PRINCE   Prithee, do, Jack.

FALSTAFF   Faith, and I'll send him packing.   [*Exit*]

PRINCE   Now, sirs, by'r lady, you fought fair, so did you, Peto, so did you, Bardolph: you are lions too, you ran away upon instinct, you will not touch the true prince; no, fie!

BARDOLPH   Faith, I ran when I saw others run.

PRINCE   Faith, tell me now in earnest, how came Falstaff's sword so hack'd?

PETO   Why, he hack'd it with his dagger, and said he would swear truth out of England, but he would make you believe it was done in fight, and persuaded us to do the like.

BARDOLPH   Yea, and to tickle our noses with spear-grass, to make them bleed, and then to beslubber our garments with it, and swear it was the blood of true men. I did that I did not this seven year before, I blush'd to hear his monstrous devices.

PRINCE   O villain, thou stolest a cup of sack eighteen years ago,

and wert taken with the manner, and ever since thou hast
blush'd extempore. Thou hadst fire and sword on thy side, and
yet thou ran'st away: what instinct hadst thou for it?

BARDOLPH My lord, do you see these meteors? do you behold
these exhalations?

PRINCE I do.

BARDOLPH What think you they portend?

PRINCE Hot livers and cold purses.

BARDOLPH Choler, my lord, if rightly taken.

PRINCE No, if rightly taken, halter.

Re-enter Falstaff

Here comes lean Jack, here comes bare-bone. How now, my
sweet creature of bombast, how long is 't ago, Jack, since thou
sawest thine own knee?

FALSTAFF My own knee? when I was about thy years, Hal, I
was not an eagles' talon in the waist, I could have crept into
any alderman's thumb-ring: a plague of sighing and grief, it
blows a man up like a bladder. There's villanous news abroad:
here was Sir John Bracy from your father; you must to the
court in the morning. That same mad fellow of the north,
Percy, and he of Wales, that gave Amamon the bastinado and
made Lucifer cuckold, and swore the devil his true liegeman
upon the cross of a Welsh hook—what a plague call you him?

POINS O, Glendower.

FALSTAFF Owen, Owen, the same, and his son-in-law Mortimer,
and old Northumberland, and that sprightly Scot of Scots,
Douglas, that runs a horseback up a hill perpendicular,—

PRINCE He that rides at high speed and with his pistol kills a
sparrow flying.

FALSTAFF You have hit it.

PRINCE So did he never the sparrow.

FALSTAFF Well, that rascal hath good mettle in him, he will
not run.

PRINCE Why, what a rascal art thou then, to praise him so for
running!

FALSTAFF   A horseback, ye cuckoo, but afoot he will not budge a foot.

PRINCE   Yes, Jack, upon instinct.

FALSTAFF   I grant ye, upon instinct. Well, he is there too, and one Mordake, and a thousand blue-caps more: Worcester is stolen away to-night, thy father's beard is turn'd white with the news, you may buy land now as cheap as stinking mackerel.

PRINCE   Why, then, it is like, if there come a hot June, and this civil buffeting hold, we shall buy maidenheads as they buy hob-nails, by the hundreds.

FALSTAFF   By the mass, lad, thou sayest true, it is like we shall have good trading that way. But tell me, Hal, art not thou horrible afeard? thou being heir-apparent, could the world pick thee out three such enemies again as that fiend Douglas, that spirit Percy, and that devil Glendower? art thou not horribly afraid? doth not thy blood thrill at it?

PRINCE   Not a whit, i' faith; I lack some of thy instinct.

FALSTAFF   Well, thou wilt be horribly chid to-morrow when thou comest to thy father: if thou love me, practise an answer.

PRINCE   Do thou stand for my father, and examine me upon the particulars of my life.

FALSTAFF   Shall I? content. This chair shall be my state, this dagger my sceptre, and this cushion my crown.

PRINCE   Thy state is taken for a joined-stool, thy golden sceptre for a leaden dagger, and thy precious rich crown for a pitiful bald crown!

FALSTAFF   Well, an the fire of grace be not quite out of thee, now shalt thou be moved. Give me a cup of sack to make my eyes look red, that it may be thought I have wept, for I must speak in passion, and I will do it in King Cambyses' vein.

PRINCE   Well, here is my leg.

FALSTAFF   And here is my speech. Stand aside, nobility.

MISTRESS QUICKLY   O Jesu, this is excellent sport, i' faith!

FALSTAFF   Weep not, sweet queen, for trickling tears are vain.

MISTRESS QUICKLY   O, the father, how he holds his countenance!

FALSTAFF   For God's sake, lords, convey my tristful queen,
For tears do stop the flood-gates of her eyes.

MISTRESS QUICKLY   O Jesu, he doth it as like one of these
harlotry players as ever I see!

FALSTAFF   Peace, good pint-pot, peace, good tickle-brain.
Harry, I do not only marvel where thou spendest thy time, but
also how thou art accompanied. For though the camomile, the
more it is trodden on, the faster it grows; so youth, the more it
is wasted, the sooner it wears. That thou art my son I have
partly thy mother's word, partly my own opinion, but chiefly
a villanous trick of thine eye, and a foolish hanging of thy
nether lip, that doth warrant me. If then thou be son to me,
here lies the point, why, being son to me, art thou so pointed
at? Shall the blessed sun of heaven prove a micher, and eat
blackberries? a question not to be ask'd. Shall the son of
England prove a thief, and take purses? a question to be ask'd.
There is a thing, Harry, which thou hast often heard of, and it
is known to many in our land by the name of pitch. This pitch
(as ancient writers do report) doth defile, so doth the company thou keepest: for, Harry, now I do not speak to thee in
drink, but in tears; not in pleasure but in passion; not in words
only, but in woes also: and yet there is a virtuous man whom
I have often noted in thy company, but I know not his
name.

PRINCE   What manner of man, an it like your majesty?

FALSTAFF   A goodly portly man, i' faith, and a corpulent, of a
cheerful look, a pleasing eye, and a most noble carriage, and, as
I think, his age some fifty, or, by'r lady, inclining to three score,
and now I remember me, his name is Falstaff, if that man should
be lewdly given, he deceiveth me. For, Harry, I see virtue in
his looks: if then the tree may be known by the fruit, as the
fruit by the tree, then peremptorily I speak it, there is virtue in
that Falstaff, him keep with, the rest banish, and tell me now,
thou naughty varlet, tell me, where hast thou been this month?

PRINCE   Dost thou speak like a king? Do thou stand for me,
and I'll play my father.

53

FALSTAFF Depose me? if thou dost it half so gravely, so majestically, both in word and matter, hang me up by the heels for a rabbit-sucker, or a poulter's hare.

PRINCE Well, here I am set.

FALSTAFF And here I stand: judge, my masters.

PRINCE Now, Harry, whence come you?

FALSTAFF My noble lord, from Eastcheap.

PRINCE The complaints I hear of thee are grievous.

FALSTAFF 'Sblood, my lord, they are false: nay, I'll tickle ye for a young prince, i' faith.

PRINCE Swearest thou, ungracious boy? henceforth ne'er look on me. Thou art violently carried away from grace, there is a devil haunts thee in the likeness of an old fat man, a tun of man is thy companion: why dost thou converse with that trunk of humours, that bolting-hutch of beastliness, that swollen parcel of dropsies, that huge bombard of sack, that stuff'd cloak-bag of guts, that roasted Manningtree ox with the pudding in his belly, that reverend vice, that grey iniquity, that father ruffian, that vanity in years? Wherein is he good, but to taste sack and drink it? wherein neat and cleanly, but to carve a capon and eat it? wherein cunning, but in craft? wherein crafty, but in villany? wherein villanous, but in all things? wherein worthy, but in nothing?

FALSTAFF I would your grace would take me with you, whom means your grace?

PRINCE That villanous abominable misleader of youth, Falstaff, that old white-bearded Satan.

FALSTAFF My lord, the man I know.

PRINCE I know thou dost.

FALSTAFF But to say I know more harm in him than in myself, were to say more than I know: that he is old (the more the pity) his white hairs do witness it, but that he is, saving your reverence, a whoremaster, that I utterly deny: if sack and sugar be a fault, God help the wicked! if to be old and merry be a sin, then many an old host that I know is damn'd: if to be fat be to be hated, then Pharaoh's lean kine are to be loved. No,

54

my good lord; banish Peto, banish Bardolph, banish Poins, but for sweet Jack Falstaff, kind Jack Falstaff, true Jack Falstaff, valiant Jack Falstaff, and therefore more valiant, being, as he is, old Jack Falstaff, banish not him thy Harry's company, banish not him thy Harry's company, banish plump Jack, and banish all the world.

PRINCE   I do, I will.   [*A knocking heard*]

[*Exeunt Mistress Quickly, Francis, and Bardolph*]

Re-enter Bardolph, running

BARDOLPH   O, my lord, my lord! the sheriff with a most monstrous watch is at the door.

FALSTAFF   Out, ye rogue! Play out the play: I have much to say in the behalf of that Falstaff.

Re-enter Mistress Quickly

MISTRESS QUICKLY   O Jesu, my lord, my lord!—

PRINCE   Heigh, heigh! the devil rides upon a fiddle-stick, what's the matter?

MISTRESS QUICKLY   The sheriff and all the watch are at the door, they are come to search the house, shall I let them in?

FALSTAFF   Dost thou hear, Hal? never call a true piece of gold a counterfeit: thou art essentially made, without seeming so.

PRINCE   And thou a natural coward, without instinct.

FALSTAFF   I deny your major: if you will deny the sheriff, so; if not, let him enter: if I become not a cart as well as another man, a plague on my bringing up! I hope I shall as soon be strangled with a halter as another.

PRINCE   Go hide thee behind the arras, the rest walk up above. Now, my masters, for a true face, and good conscience.

FALSTAFF   Both which I have had, but their date is out, and therefore I'll hide me.

PRINCE   Call in the sheriff.

[*Exeunt all except the Prince and Peto*]

Enter Sheriff and the Carrier

Now, master sheriff, what is your will with me?

55

ACT II SCENE 4

SHERIFF First pardon me, my lord. A hue and cry
Hath follow'd certain men unto this house.
PRINCE What men?
SHERIFF One of them is well known, my gracious lord,
A gross fat man.
CARRIER As fat as butter.
PRINCE The man, I do assure you, is not here,
For I myself at this time have employ'd him.
And, sheriff, I will engage my word to thee
That I will by to-morrow dinner-time
Send him to answer thee or any man,
For any thing he shall be charg'd withal,
And so let me entreat you leave the house.
SHERIFF I will, my lord. There are two gentlemen
Have in this robbery lost three hundred marks.
PRINCE It may be so: if he have robb'd these men,
He shall be answerable, and so farewell.
SHERIFF Good night, my noble lord.
PRINCE I think it is good morrow, is it not?
SHERIFF Indeed, my lord, I think it be two o'clock.
                                    [Exeunt Sheriff and Carrier]
PRINCE This oily rascal is known as well as Paul's.
Go, call him forth.
PETO Falstaff!—Fast asleep behind the arras, and snorting like
a horse.
PRINCE Hark how hard he fetches breath; search his pockets.
(He searcheth his pockets, and findeth certain papers.) What hast thou
found?
PETO Nothing but papers, my lord.
PRINCE Let's see what they be: read them.
PETO (reads) Item a capon, . . . 2s. 2d.
Item sauce, ... 4d.
Item sack two gallons, . . 5s. 8d.
Item anchovies and sack after
supper, ... 2s. 6d.
Item bread, ... 0½d.

56

PRINCE O monstrous! but one half-pennyworth of bread to this
intolerable deal of sack! What there is else keep close, we'll
read it at more advantage: there let him sleep till day; I'll to
the court in the morning. We must all to the wars, and thy
place shall be honourable. I'll procure this fat rogue a charge
of foot, and I know his death will be a march of twelve-score;
the money shall be paid back again with advantage; be with
me betimes in the morning, and so good morrow, Peto.
PETO Good morrow, good my lord.   [*Exeunt*]

ACT THIRD

Scene One: **Bangor. The Archdeacon's House**

Enter Hotspur, Worcester, Mortimer, and Glendower

MORTIMER   These promises are fair, the parties sure,
And our induction full of prosperous hope.
HOTSPUR   Lord Mortimer, and cousin Glendower,
Will you sit down? And uncle Worcester:
A plague upon it, I have forgot the map.
GLENDOWER   No, here it is. Sit, cousin Percy, sit,
Good cousin Hotspur, for by that name
As oft as Lancaster doth speak of you,
His cheek looks pale, and with a rising sigh
He wisheth you in heaven.
HOTSPUR   And you in hell,
As oft as he hears Owen Glendower spoke of.
GLENDOWER   I cannot blame him: at my nativity
The front of heaven was full of fiery shapes,
Of burning cressets, and at my birth
The frame and huge foundation of the earth
Shak'd like a coward.
HOTSPUR   Why, so it would have done
At the same season, if your mother's cat
Had but kitten'd, though yourself had ne'er been born.
GLENDOWER   I say the earth did shake when I was born.
HOTSPUR   And I say the earth was not of my mind,
If you suppose as fearing you it shook.
GLENDOWER   The heavens were all on fire, the earth did
tremble.
HOTSPUR   O, then the earth shook to see the heavens on fire,
And not in fear of your nativity.
Diseased nature oftentimes breaks forth,
In strange eruptions; oft the teeming earth

Is with a kind of colic pinch'd and vex'd,
By the imprisoning of unruly wind
Within her womb, which, for enlargement striving,
Shakes the old beldam earth, and topples down
Steeples and moss-grown towers. At your birth
Our grandam earth, having this distemperature,
In passion shook.
GLENDOWER   Cousin, of many men
I do not bear these crossings; give me leave
To tell you once again that at my birth
The front of heaven was full of fiery shapes,
The goats ran from the mountains, and the herds
Were strangely clamorous to the frighted fields.
These signs have mark'd me extraordinary,
And all the courses of my life do show
I am not in the roll of common men.
Where is he living, clipp'd in with the sea
That chides the banks of England, Scotland, Wales,
Which calls me pupil, or hath read to me?
And bring him out that is but woman's son
Can trace me in the tedious ways of art,
And hold me pace in deep experiments.
HOTSPUR   I think there is no man speaks better Welsh.
I'll to dinner.
MORTIMER   Peace, cousin Percy, you will make him mad.
GLENDOWER   I can call spirits from the vasty deep.
HOTSPUR   Why, so can I, or so can any man,
But will they come when you do call for them?
GLENDOWER   Why, I can teach you, cousin, to command the
devil.
HOTSPUR   And I can teach thee, coz, to shame the devil,
By telling truth. Tell truth, and shame the devil.
If thou have power to raise him, bring him hither,
And I'll be sworn I have power to shame him hence.
O, while you live, tell truth, and shame the devil!
MORTIMER   Come, come, no more of this unprofitable chat.

59

GLENDOWER   Three times hath Henry Bolingbroke made head
  Against my power, thrice from the banks of Wye
  And sandy-bottom'd Severn have I sent
  Him bootless home and weather-beaten back.
HOTSPUR   Home without boots, and in foul weather too!
  How 'scapes he agues, in the devil's name?
GLENDOWER   Come, here's the map: shall we divide our right
  According to our threefold order ta'en?
MORTIMER   The archdeacon hath divided it
  Into three limits very equally:
  England, from Trent, and Severn hitherto,
  By south and east is to my part assign'd:
  All westward, Wales beyond the Severn shore,
  And all the fertile land within that bound,
  To Owen Glendower: and, dear coz, to you
  The remnant northward, lying off from Trent.
  And our indentures tripartite are drawn;
  Which being sealed interchangeably,
  (A business that this night may execute,)
  To-morrow, cousin Percy, you and I
  And my good Lord of Worcester will set forth
  To meet your father and the Scottish power,
  As is appointed us, at Shrewsbury.
  My father Glendower is not ready yet,
  Nor shall we need his help these fourteen days.
  Within that space you may have drawn together
  Your tenants, friends, and neighbouring gentlemen.
GLENDOWER   A shorter time shall send me to you, lords:
  And in my conduct shall your ladies come,
  From whom you now must steal and take no leave,
  For there will be a world of water shed
  Upon the parting of your wives and you.
HOTSPUR   Methinks my moiety, north from Burton here,
  In quantity equals not one of yours:
  See how this river comes me cranking in,
  And cuts me from the best of all my land

He holds your temper in a high respect,
And curbs himself even of his natural scope
When you come 'cross his humour; faith, he does:
I warrant you, that man is not alive
Might so have tempted him as you have done,
Without the taste of danger and reproof:
But do not use it oft, let me entreat you.
WORCESTER   In faith, my lord, you are too wilful-blame,
And since your coming hither have done enough
To put him quite beside his patience;
You must needs learn, lord, to amend this fault:
Though sometimes it show greatness, courage, blood,—
And that's the dearest grace it renders you,—
Yet oftentimes it doth present harsh rage,
Defect of manners, want of government,
Pride, haughtiness, opinion, and disdain,
The least of which haunting a noble man
Loseth men's hearts, and leaves behind a stain
Upon the beauty of all parts besides,
Beguiling them of commendation.
HOTSPUR   Well, I am school'd: good manners be your speed!
Here come our wives, and let us take our leave.

Re-enter Glendower with the ladies

MORTIMER   This is the deadly spite that angers me;
My wife can speak no English, I no Welsh.
GLENDOWER   My daughter weeps: she'll not part with you;
She'll be a soldier too, she'll to the wars.
MORTIMER   Good father, tell her that she and my aunt Percy
Shall follow in your conduct speedily.
[*Glendower speaks to her in Welsh, and she answers him in the same*]
GLENDOWER   She is desperate here; a peevish self-will'd
harlotry, one that no persuasion can do good upon.
[*The lady speaks in Welsh*]

63

MORTIMER   I understand thy looks: that pretty Welsh
    Which thou pourest down from these swelling heavens
    I am too perfect in; and, but for shame,
    In such a parley should I answer thee.
                            [The lady speaks again in Welsh]
    I understand thy kisses, and thou mine,
    And that's a feeling disputation:
    But I will never be a truant, love,
    Till I have learn'd thy language, for thy tongue
    Makes Welsh as sweet as ditties highly penn'd,
    Sung by a fair queen in a summer's bower,
    With ravishing division, to her lute.
GLENDOWER   Nay, if you melt, then will she run mad.
                            [The lady speaks again in Welsh]
MORTIMER   O, I am ignorance itself in this!
GLENDOWER   She bids you on the wanton rushes lay you down
    And rest your gentle head upon her lap,
    And she will sing the song that pleaseth you,
    And on your eyelids crown the god of sleep,
    Charming your blood with pleasing heaviness,
    Making such difference 'twixt wake and sleep
    As is the difference betwixt day and night,
    The hour before the heavenly-harness'd team
    Begins his golden progress in the east.
MORTIMER   With all my heart I'll sit and hear her sing:
    By that time will our book, I think, be drawn.
GLENDOWER   Do so;
    And those musicians that shall play to you
    Hang in the air a thousand leagues from hence,
    And straight they shall be here: sit, and attend.
HOTSPUR   Come, Kate, thou art perfect in lying down:
    Come quick, quick, that I may lay my head in thy lap.
LADY PERCY   Go, ye giddy goose.   *[The music plays]*
HOTSPUR   Now I perceive the devil understands Welsh:
    And 'tis no marvel he is so humorous.
    By'r lady, he is a good musician.

LADY PERCY   Then should you be nothing but musical, for you
are altogether governed by humours. Lie still, ye thief, and hear
the lady sing in Welsh.

HOTSPUR   I had rather hear Lady, my brach, howl in Irish.

LADY PERCY   Wouldst thou have thy head broken?

HOTSPUR   No.

LADY PERCY   Then be still.

HOTSPUR   Neither, 'tis a woman's fault.

LADY PERCY   Now God help thee!

HOTSPUR   To the Welsh lady's bed.

LADY PERCY   What's that?

HOTSPUR   Peace! she sings.   [*Here the lady sings a Welsh song*]

HOTSPUR   Come, Kate, I'll have your song too.

LADY PERCY   Not mine, in good sooth.

HOTSPUR   Not yours, in good sooth! Heart! you swear like a
comfit-maker's wife. 'Not you, in good sooth,' and 'as true as I
live,' and 'as God shall mend me,' and 'as sure as day,'
And givest such sarcenet surety for thy oaths,
As if thou never walk'st further than Finsbury.
Swear me, Kate, like a lady as thou art,
A good mouth-filling oath, and leave 'in sooth,'
And such protest of pepper-gingerbread,
To velvet-guards and Sunday-citizens.
Come, sing.

LADY PERCY   I will not sing.

HOTSPUR   'Tis the next way to turn tailor, or be redbreast
teacher. An the indentures be drawn, I'll away within these
two hours, and so come in when ye will.   [*Exit*]

GLENDOWER   Come, come, Lord Mortimer; you are as slow
As hot Lord Percy is on fire to go.
By this our book is drawn, we'll but seal, and then
To horse immediately.

MORTIMER   With all my heart.

                                        [*Exeunt*]

Scene Two: **London. The Palace**

Enter the King, Prince of Wales, and others

KING   Lords, give us leave; the Prince of Wales and I
   Must have some private conference, but be near at hand,
   For we shall presently have need of you.

                                              [*Exeunt Lords*]

   I know not whether God will have it so,
   For some displeasing service I have done,
   That, in his secret doom, out of my blood
   He'll breed revengement and a scourge for me;
   But thou dost in thy passages of life
   Make me believe that thou art only mark'd
   For the hot vengeance, and the rod of heaven,
   To punish my mistreadings. Tell me else,
   Could such inordinate and low desires,
   Such poor, such bare, such lewd, such mean attempts,
   Such barren pleasures, rude society,
   As thou art match'd withal, and grafted to,
   Accompany the greatness of thy blood,
   And hold their level with thy princely heart?
PRINCE   So please your majesty, I would I could
   Quit all offences with as clear excuse
   As well as I am doubtless I can purge
   Myself of many I am charg'd withal;
   Yet such extenuation let me beg,
   As, in reproof of many tales devis'd,
   Which oft the ear of greatness needs must hear,
   By smiling pick-thanks, and base newsmongers,
   I may, for some things true, wherein my youth
   Hath faulty wander'd, and irregular,
   Find pardon on my true submission.
KING   God pardon thee! yet let me wonder, Harry,
   At thy affections, which do hold a wing
   Quite from the flight of all thy ancestors.

Thy place in council thou hast rudely lost,
Which by thy younger brother is supplied,
And art almost an alien to the hearts
Of all the court and princes of my blood:
The hope and expectation of thy time
Is ruin'd, and the soul of every man
Prophetically do forethink thy fall.
Had I so lavish of my presence been,
So common-hackney'd in the eyes of men,
So stale and cheap to vulgar company,
Opinion, that did help me to the crown,
Had still kept loyal to possession,
And left me in reputeless banishment,
A fellow of no mark nor likelihood.
By being seldom seen, I could not stir
But like a comet I was wonder'd at;
That men would tell their children 'This is he;'
Others would say 'Where, which is Bolingbroke?'
And then I stole all courtesy from heaven,
And dress'd myself in such humility
That I did pluck allegiance from men's hearts,
Loud shouts and salutations from their mouths,
Even in the presence of the crowned king.
Thus did I keep my person fresh and new;
My presence like a robe pontifical,
Ne'er seen but wonder'd at, and so my state,
Seldom but sumptuous, showed like a feast,
And won by rareness such solemnity.
The skipping king, he ambled up and down,
With shallow jesters, and rash bavin wits,
Soon kindled, and soon burnt; carded his state,
Mingled his royalty with capering fools,
Had his great name profaned with their scorns,
And gave his countenance, against his name,
To laugh at gibing boys, and stand the push
Of every beardless vain comparative,

Grew a companion to the common streets,
Enfeoff'd himself to popularity,
That, being daily swallow'd by men's eyes,
They surfeited with honey, and began
To loathe the taste of sweetness, whereof a little
More than a little is by much too much.
So when he had occasion to be seen,
He was but as the cuckoo is in June,
Heard, not regarded; seen, but with such eyes
As, sick and blunted with community,
Afford no extraordinary gaze,
Such as is bent on sun-like majesty
When it shines seldom in admiring eyes,
But rather drowz'd, and hung their eyelids down,
Slept in his face, and render'd such aspect
As cloudy men use to their adversaries,
Being with his presence glutted, gorg'd, and full.
And in that very line, Harry, standest thou,
For thou hast lost thy princely privilege
With vile participation. Not an eye
But is a-weary of thy common sight,
Save mine, which hath desir'd to see thee more,
Which now doth that I would not have it do,
Make blind itself with foolish tenderness.

PRINCE   I shall hereafter, my thrice gracious lord,
Be more myself.

KING   For all the world
As thou art to this hour was Richard then,
When I from France set foot at Ravenspurgh,
And even as I was then, is Percy now.
Now, by my sceptre, and my soul to boot,
He hath more worthy interest to the state
Than thou the shadow of succession;
For of no right, nor colour like to right,
He doth fill fields with harness in the realm,
Turns head against the lion's armed jaws,

68

And, being no more in debt to years than thou,
Leads ancient lords and reverend bishops on
To bloody battles and to bruising arms.
What never-dying honour hath he got
Against renowned Douglas! whose high deeds,
Whose hot incursions, and great name in arms,
Holds from all soldiers chief majority
And military title capital
Through all the kingdoms that acknowledge Christ:
Thrice hath this Hotspur Mars in swathling clothes,
This infant warrior, in his enterprizes
Discomfited great Douglas, ta'en him once,
Enlarged him, and made a friend of him,
To fill the mouth of deep defiance up,
And shake the peace and safety of our throne.
And what say you to this? Percy, Northumberland,
The Archbishop's grace of York, Douglas, Mortimer,
Capitulate against us, and are up.
But wherefore do I tell these news to thee?
Why, Harry, do I tell thee of my foes,
Which art my nearest and dearest enemy?
Thou that art like enough through vassal fear,
Base inclination, and the start of spleen,
To fight against me under Percy's pay,
To dog his heels, and curtsy at his frowns,
To show how much thou art degenerate.
PRINCE   Do not think so, you shall not find it so,
And God forgive them that so much have sway'd
Your majesty's good thoughts away from me!
I will redeem all this on Percy's head,
And in the closing of some glorious day
Be bold to tell you that I am your son,
When I will wear a garment all of blood,
And stain my favours in a bloody mask,
Which, wash'd away, shall scour my shame with it,
And that shall be the day, whene'er it lights,

That this same child of honour and renown,
This gallant Hotspur, this all-praised knight,
And your unthought-of Harry chance to meet.
For every honour sitting on his helm,
Would they were multitudes, and on my head
My shames redoubled! For the time will come
That I shall make this northern youth exchange
His glorious deeds for my indignities.
Percy is but my factor, good my lord,
To engross up glorious deeds on my behalf;
And I will call him to so strict account,
That he shall render every glory up,
Yea, even the slightest worship of his time,
Or I will tear the reckoning from his heart.
This in the name of God I promise here:
The which if He be pleased I shall perform,
I do beseech your majesty may salve
The long-grown wounds of my intemperance:
If not, the end of life cancels all bands,
And I will die a hundred thousand deaths
Ere break the smallest parcel of this vow.
KING   A hundred thousand rebels die in this;
Thou shalt have charge and sovereign trust herein.

Enter Blunt

How now, good Blunt? thy looks are full of speed.
BLUNT   So hath the business that I come to speak of.
Lord Mortimer of Scotland hath sent word
That Douglas and the English rebels met
The eleventh of this month at Shrewsbury;
A mighty and a fearful head they are,
If promises be kept on every hand,
As ever offer'd foul play in a state.
KING   The Earl of Westmoreland set forth to-day,
With him my son, Lord John of Lancaster,
For this advertisement is five days old:

On Wednesday next, Harry, you shall set forward,
On Thursday we ourselves will march.
Our meeting is Bridgenorth, and, Harry, you
Shall march through Gloucestershire, by which account,
Our business valued, some twelve days hence
Our general forces at Bridgenorth shall meet.
Our hands are full of business, let's away;
Advantage feeds him fat while men delay.   [*Exeunt*]

Scene Three: **The Boar's-Head Tavern in Eastcheap**

Enter Falstaff and Bardolph

FALSTAFF   Bardolph, am I not fallen away vilely since this last
action? do I not bate? do I not dwindle? Why, my skin hangs
about me like an old lady's loose gown. I am withered like an
old apple-john. Well, I'll repent, and that suddenly, while I am
in some liking; I shall be out of heart shortly, and then I shall
have no strength to repent. An I have not forgotten what the
inside of a church is made of, I am a peppercorn, a brewer's
horse: the inside of a church! Company, villanous company,
hath been the spoil of me.

BARDOLPH   Sir John, you are so fretful, you cannot live long.

FALSTAFF   Why, there is it: come sing me a bawdy song, make
me merry. I was as virtuously given as a gentleman need to be,
virtuous enough, swore little, dic'd not above seven times a
week, went to a bawdy-house not above once in a quarter of
an hour, paid money that I borrowed three or four times, lived
well, and in good compass, and now I live out of all order, out
of all compass.

BARDOLPH   Why, you are so fat, Sir John, that you must needs
be out of all compass; out of all reasonable compass, Sir John.

FALSTAFF   Do thou amend thy face, and I'll amend my life:
thou art our admiral, thou bearest the lantern in the poop,

71

but 'tis in the nose of thee; thou art the Knight of the Burning Lamp.

BARDOLPH Why, Sir John, my face does you no harm.

FALSTAFF No, I'll be sworn, I make as good use of it as many a man doth of a Death's-head, or a *memento mori*. I never see thy face but I think upon hell-fire, and Dives that lived in purple: for there he is in his robes, burning, burning. If thou wert any way given to virtue, I would swear by thy face; my oath should be, 'By this fire, that's God's angel.' But thou art altogether given over; and wert indeed, but for the light in thy face, the son of utter darkness. When thou ran'st up Gadshill in the night to catch my horse, if I did not think thou hadst been an *ignis fatuus*, or a ball of wildfire, there's no purchase in money. O, thou art a perpetual triumph, an everlasting bonfire-light, thou hast saved me a thousand marks in links and torches, walking with thee in the night betwixt tavern and tavern; but the sack that thou hast drunk me, would have bought me lights as good cheap, at the dearest chandler's in Europe. I have maintained that salamander of yours with fire any time this two and thirty years, God reward me for it!

BARDOLPH 'Sblood, I would my face were in your belly!

FALSTAFF God-a-mercy, so should I be sure to be heart-burn'd!

Enter Mistress Quickly

How now, Dame Partlet the hen, have you inquir'd yet who pick'd my pocket?

MISTRESS QUICKLY Why, Sir John, what do you think, Sir John? do you think I keep thieves in my house? I have search'd, I have inquir'd, so has my husband, man by man, boy by boy, servant by servant; the tithe of a hair was never lost in my house before.

FALSTAFF Ye lie, hostess: Bardolph was shav'd, and lost many a hair, and I'll be sworn my pocket was pick'd: go to, you are a woman, go.

MISTRESS QUICKLY Who, I? no; I defy thee: God's light, I was never call'd so in mine own house before.

72

FALSTAFF Go to, I know you well enough.

MISTRESS QUICKLY No, Sir John, you do not know me, Sir John, I know you, Sir John, you owe me money, Sir John, and now you pick a quarrel to beguile me of it, I bought you a dozen of shirts to your back.

FALSTAFF Dowlas, filthy dowlas: I have given them away to bakers' wives, they have made bolters of them.

MISTRESS QUICKLY Now, as I am a true woman, holland of eight shillings an ell, you owe money here besides, Sir John, for your diet, and by-drinkings, and money lent you, four and twenty pound.

FALSTAFF He had his part of it, let him pay.

MISTRESS QUICKLY He? alas, he is poor, he hath nothing.

FALSTAFF How? poor? look upon his face. What call you rich? let them coin his nose, let them coin his cheeks, I'll not pay a denier. What, will you make a younker of me? shall I not take mine ease in mine inn, but I shall have my pocket pick'd? I have lost a seal-ring of my grandfather's worth forty mark.

MISTRESS QUICKLY O Jesu, I have heard the prince tell him, I know not how oft, that that ring was copper!

FALSTAFF How? the prince is a Jack, a sneak-cup: 'sblood, an he were here, I would cudgel him like a dog, if he would say so.

Enter the Prince and Peto, marching, and Falstaff meets them playing on his truncheon like a fife

How now, lad? is the wind in that door, i' faith? must we all march?

BARDOLPH Yea, two and two, Newgate fashion.

MISTRESS QUICKLY My lord, I pray you, hear me.

PRINCE What sayest thou, Mistress Quickly? How doth thy husband? I love him well, he is an honest man.

MISTRESS QUICKLY Good my lord, hear me.

FALSTAFF Prithee let her alone, and list to me.

PRINCE What say'st thou, Jack?

FALSTAFF The other night I fell asleep here, behind the arras, and had my pocket pick'd; this house is turn'd bawdy-house, they pick pockets.

PRINCE What didst thou lose, Jack?

FALSTAFF Wilt thou believe me, Hal, three or four bonds of forty pound a-piece, and a seal-ring of my grandfather's.

PRINCE A trifle, some eight-penny matter.

MISTRESS QUICKLY So I told him, my lord, and I said I heard your grace say so: and, my lord, he speaks most vilely of you, like a foul-mouth'd man as he is, and said he would cudgel you.

PRINCE What! he did not?

MISTRESS QUICKLY There's neither faith, truth, nor womanhood in me else.

FALSTAFF There's no more faith in thee than in a stew'd prune, nor no more truth in thee than in a drawn fox, and for womanhood, Maid Marian may be the deputy's wife of the ward to thee. Go, you thing, go.

MISTRESS QUICKLY Say, what thing? what thing?

FALSTAFF What thing? why, a thing to thank God on.

MISTRESS QUICKLY I am no thing to thank God on, I would thou shouldst know it, I am an honest man's wife, and, setting thy knighthood aside, thou art a knave to call me so.

FALSTAFF Setting thy womanhood aside, thou art a beast to say otherwise.

MISTRESS QUICKLY Say, what beast, thou knave, thou?

FALSTAFF What beast? why, an otter.

PRINCE An otter, Sir John, why an otter?

FALSTAFF Why? she's neither fish nor flesh, a man knows not where to have her.

MISTRESS QUICKLY Thou art an unjust man in saying so, thou or any man knows where to have me, thou knave, thou!

PRINCE Thou sayst true, hostess, and he slanders thee most grossly.

MISTRESS QUICKLY So he doth you, my lord, and said this other day you ought him a thousand pound.

PRINCE Sirrah, do I owe you a thousand pound?

FALSTAFF A thousand pound, Hal? a million, thy love is worth a million, thou owest me thy love.

MISTRESS QUICKLY Nay, my lord, he called you Jack, and said he would cudgel you.

FALSTAFF Did I Bardolph?

BARDOLPH Indeed, Sir John, you said so.

FALSTAFF Yea, if he said my ring was copper.

PRINCE I say 'tis copper, darest thou be as good as thy word now?

FALSTAFF Why, Hal! Thou knowest as thou art but man I dare, but as thou art prince, I fear thee as I fear the roaring of the lion's whelp.

PRINCE And why not as the lion?

FALSTAFF The king himself is to be feared as the lion; dost thou think I'll fear thee as I fear thy father? nay, an I do, I pray God my girdle break.

PRINCE O, if it should, how would thy guts fall about thy knees! But, sirrah, there's no room for faith, truth, nor honesty in this bosom of thine; it is all fill'd up with guts, and midriff. Charge an honest woman with picking thy pocket! why, thou whoreson, impudent, emboss'd rascal, if there were anything in thy pocket but tavern-reckonings, memorandums of bawdy-houses, and one poor penny-worth of sugar-candy to make thee long-winded, if thy pocket were enrich'd with any other injuries but these, I am a villain; and yet you will stand to it, you will not pocket up wrong; art thou not ashamed?

FALSTAFF Dost thou hear, Hal? thou knowest in the state of innocency Adam fell, and what should poor Jack Falstaff do in the days of villany? Thou seest I have more flesh than another man, and therefore more frailty. You confess then, you pick'd my pocket?

PRINCE It appears so by the story.

FALSTAFF Hostess, I forgive thee, go, make ready breakfast, love thy husband, look to thy servants, cherish thy guests, thou shalt find me tractable to any honest reason, thou seest I am pacified still. Nay, prithee be gone. (*Exit Mistress Quickly.*)

Now, Hal, to the news at court; for the robbery, lad, how is that answered?

PRINCE   O, my sweet beef, I must still be good angel to thee; the money is paid back again.

FALSTAFF   O, I do not like that paying back, 'tis a double labour.

PRINCE   I am good friends with my father, and may do any thing.

FALSTAFF   Rob me the exchequer the first thing thou doest, and do it with unwash'd hands too.

BARDOLPH   Do, my lord.

PRINCE   I have procured thee, Jack, a charge of foot.

FALSTAFF   I would it had been of horse. Where shall I find one that can steal well? O for a fine thief, of the age of two and twenty or thereabouts! I am heinously unprovided. Well, God be thanked for these rebels, they offend none but the virtuous; I laud them, I praise them.

PRINCE   Bardolph!

BARDOLPH   My lord?

PRINCE   Go bear this letter to Lord John of Lancaster,
To my brother John; this to my Lord of Westmoreland.
                                                    [*Exit Bardolph*]
Go, Peto, to horse, to horse, for thou and I
Have thirty miles to ride yet ere dinner time.   [*Exit Peto*]
Jack, meet me to-morrow in the Temple hall
At two o'clock in the afternoon.
There shalt thou know thy charge, and there receive
Money and order for their furniture.
The land is burning; Percy stands on high;
And either we or they must lower lie.   [*Exit*]

FALSTAFF   Rare words! brave world! Hostess, my breakfast, come!
O, I could wish this tavern were my drum!   [*Exit*]

Mistress Quickly

ACT FOURTH

Scene One: **The Rebel Camp near Shrewsbury**

Enter Hotspur, Worcester, and Douglas

HOTSPUR Well said, my noble Scot: if speaking truth
In this fine age were not thought flattery,
Such attribution should the Douglas have,
As not a soldier of this season's stamp
Should go so general current through the world.
By God, I cannot flatter, I do defy
The tongues of soothers, but a braver place
In my heart's love hath no man than yourself:
Nay, task me to my word, approve me, lord.
DOUGLAS Thou art the king of honour:
No man so potent breathes upon the ground
But I will beard him.
HOTSPUR   Do so, and 'tis well.

Enter a Messenger with letters

What letters hast thou there?—I can but thank you.
MESSENGER These letters come from your father.
HOTSPUR Letters from him? why comes he not himself?
MESSENGER He cannot come, my lord, he is grievous sick.
HOTSPUR 'Zounds, how has he the leisure to be sick
In such a justling time? Who leads his power?
Under whose government come they along?
MESSENGER His letters bear his mind, not I, my lord.
WORCESTER I prithee tell me, doth he keep his bed?
MESSENGER He did, my lord, four days ere I set forth,
And at the time of my departure thence
He was much fear'd by his physicians.
WORCESTER I would the state of time had first been whole,
Ere he by sickness had been visited;

His health was never better worth than now.

HOTSPUR Sick now! droop now! this sickness doth infect
The very life-blood of our enterprise;
'Tis catching hither, even to our camp;
He writes me here, that inward sickness—
And that his friends by deputation could not
So soon be drawn, nor did he think it meet
To lay so dangerous and dear a trust
On any soul remov'd but on his own—
Yet doth he give us bold advertisement,
That with our small conjunction we should on,
To see how fortune is dispos'd to us,
For, as he writes, there is no quailing now,
Because the king is certainly possess'd
Of all our purposes. What say you to it?

WORCESTER Your father's sickness is a maim to us.

HOTSPUR A perilous gash, a very limb lopp'd off:
And yet, in faith, it is not; his present want
Seems more than we shall find it: were it good
To set the exact wealth of all our states
All at one cast? to set so rich a main
On the nice hazard of one doubtful hour?
It were not good; for therein should we read
The very bottom and the soul of hope,
The very list, the very utmost bound
Of all our fortunes.

DOUGLAS   Faith, and so we should;
Where now remains a sweet reversion:
We may boldly spend upon the hope of what
Is to come in:
A comfort of retirement lives in this.

HOTSPUR A rendezvous, a home to fly unto,
If that the devil and mischance look big
Upon the maidenhead of our affairs.

WORCESTER But yet I would your father had been here.
The quality and hair of our attempt

Brooks no division, it will be thought
By some, that know not why he is away,
That wisdom, loyalty and mere dislike
Of our proceedings kept the earl from hence:
And think how such an apprehension
May turn the tide of fearful faction,
And breed a kind of question in our cause;
For well you know we of the offering side
Must keep aloof from strict arbitrement,
And stop all sight-holes, every loop, from whence
The eye of reason may pry in upon us:
This absence of your father's draws a curtain,
That shows the ignorant a kind of fear
Before not dreamt of.

HOTSPUR   You strain too far.
I rather of his absence make this use,
It lends a lustre and more great opinion,
A larger dare to our great enterprise,
Than if the earl were here, for men must think,
If we without his help can make a head
To push against a kingdom, with his help
We shall o'erturn it topsy-turvy down;
Yet all goes well, yet all our joints are whole.

DOUGLAS   As heart can think; there is not such a word
Spoke of in Scotland as this term of fear.

Enter Sir Richard Vernon

HOTSPUR   My cousin Vernon, welcome, by my soul!

VERNON   Pray God my news be worth a welcome, lord.
The Earl of Westmoreland, seven thousand strong,
Is marching hitherwards, with him Prince John.

HOTSPUR   No harm; what more?

VERNON   And further, I have learn'd,
The king himself in person is set forth,
Or hitherwards intended speedily,
With strong and mighty preparation.

HOTSPUR   He shall be welcome too. Where is his son,
　　The nimble-footed madcap Prince of Wales,
　　And his comrades, that daff'd the world aside,
　　And bid it pass?
VERNON　　　　　All furnish'd, all in arms;
　　All plum'd like estridges that with the wind
　　Baited like eagles having lately bath'd,
　　Glittering in golden coats, like images,
　　As full of spirit as the month of May,
　　And gorgeous as the sun at midsummer;
　　Wanton as youthful goats, wild as young bulls.
　　I saw young Harry, with his beaver on,
　　His cuisses on his thighs, gallantly arm'd,
　　Rise from the ground like feather'd Mercury,
　　And vaulted with such ease into his seat,
　　As if an angel dropp'd down from the clouds,
　　To turn and wind a fiery Pegasus,
　　And witch the world with noble horsemanship.
HOTSPUR   No more, no more: worse than the sun in March,
　　This praise doth nourish agues. Let them come;
　　They come like sacrifices in their trim,
　　And to the fire-ey'd maid of smoky war
　　All hot and bleeding will we offer them:
　　The mailed Mars shall on his altars sit
　　Up to the ears in blood. I am on fire
　　To hear this rich reprisal is so nigh
　　And yet not ours. Come, let me taste my horse,
　　Who is to bear me like a thunderbolt
　　Against the bosom of the Prince of Wales:
　　Harry to Harry shall, hot horse to horse,
　　Meet and ne'er part till one drop down a corse.
　　O that Glendower were come!
VERNON　　　　　　　　　There is more news:
　　I learn'd in Worcester, as I rode along,
　　He cannot draw his power this fourteen days.
DOUGLAS   That's the worst tidings that I hear of yet.

WORCESTER Ay, by my faith, that bears a frosty sound.
HOTSPUR What may the king's whole battle reach unto?
VERNON To thirty thousand.
HOTSPUR   Forty let it be:
  My father and Glendower being both away,
  The powers of us may serve so great a day.
  Come, let us take a muster speedily:
  Doomsday is near; die all, die merrily.
DOUGLAS Talk not of dying; I am out of fear
  Of death or death's hand for this one half year.   [*Exeunt*]

Scene Two: **A Public Road near Coventry**

Enter Falstaff and Bardolph

FALSTAFF Bardolph, get thee before to Coventry, fill me a
  bottle of sack, our soldiers shall march through; we'll to Sutton
  Cop-hill to-night.
BARDOLPH Will you give me money, captain?
FALSTAFF Lay out, lay out.
BARDOLPH This bottle makes an angel.
FALSTAFF An if it do, take it for thy labour, an if it make
  twenty, take them all; I'll answer the coinage. Bid my lieu-
  tenant Peto meet me at town's end.
BARDOLPH I will, captain: farewell.   [*Exit*]
FALSTAFF If I be not ashamed of my soldiers, I am a sous'd
  gurnet; I have misused the king's press damnably. I have got
  in exchange of a hundred and fifty soldiers three hundred and
  odd pounds. I press me none but good householders, yeomen's
  sons, inquire me out contracted bachelors, such as had been
  asked twice on the banns, such a commodity of warm slaves, as
  had as lieve hear the devil as a drum, such as fear the report of
  a caliver worse than a struck fowl, or a hurt wild-duck. I press'd
  me none but such toasts-and-butter, with hearts in their bellies
  no bigger than pins'-heads and they have bought out their
  services, and now my whole charge consists of ancients, cor-

porals, lieutenants, gentlemen of companies; slaves as ragged as
Lazarus in the painted cloth, where the glutton's dogs licked
his sores, and such as indeed were never soldiers, but discarded
unjust serving-men, younger sons to younger brothers, revolted
tapsters, and ostlers, trade-fallen, the cankers of a calm world
and a long peace, ten times more dishonourable ragged than
an old fac'd ancient, and such have I to fill up the rooms of
them that have bought out their services, that you would think
that I had a hundred and fifty tattered prodigals, lately come
from swine-keeping, from eating draff and husks. A mad fellow
met me on the way, and told me I had unloaded all the gibbets,
and press'd the dead bodies. No eye hath seen such scarecrows.
I'll not march through Coventry with them, that's flat: nay,
and the villains march wide betwixt the legs, as if they had
gyves on, for indeed I had the most of them out of prison; there's
not a shirt and a half in all my company, and the half shirt is
two napkins tack'd together, and thrown over the shoulders like
a herald's coat without sleeves, and the shirt, to say the truth,
stolen from my host at Saint Alban's, or the red-nose innkeeper
of Daventry, but that's all one, they'll find linen enough on every
hedge.

Enter the Prince and Westmoreland

PRINCE   How now, blown Jack? how now, quilt?

FALSTAFF   What, Hal, how now, mad wag? what a devil dost
thou in Warwickshire? My good Lord of Westmoreland, I cry
you mercy, I thought your honour had already been at Shrewsbury.

WESTMORELAND   Faith, Sir John, 'tis more than time that I
were there, and you too, but my powers are there already; the
king, I can tell you, looks for us all, we must away all night.

FALSTAFF   Tut, never fear me, I am as vigilant as a cat to steal
cream.

PRINCE   I think, to steal cream indeed, for thy theft hath already
made thee butter; but tell me, Jack, whose fellows are these
that come after?

FALSTAFF   Mine, Hal, mine.

PRINCE   I did never see such pitiful rascals.

FALSTAFF   Tut, tut, good enough to toss, food for powder, food for powder, they'll fill a pit as well as better: tush, man, mortal men, mortal men.

WESTMORELAND   Ay, but, Sir John, methinks they are exceeding poor and bare, too beggarly.

FALSTAFF   Faith, for their poverty, I know not where they had that, and for their bareness, I am sure they never learn'd that of me.

PRINCE   No, I'll be sworn, unless you call three fingers on the ribs bare; but, sirrah, make haste, Percy is already in the field.
                                                                                            [*Exit*]

FALSTAFF   What, is the king encamp'd?

WESTMORELAND   He is, Sir John, I fear we shall stay too long.

FALSTAFF   Well,
    To the latter end of a fray, and the beginning of a feast,
    Fits a dull fighter and a keen guest.   [*Exeunt*]

Scene Three: **The Rebel Camp near Shrewsbury**

Enter Hotspur, Worcester, Douglas, and Vernon

HOTSPUR   We'll fight with him to-night.

WORCESTER   It may not be.

DOUGLAS   You give him then advantage.

VERNON   Not a whit.

HOTSPUR   Why say you so? looks he not for supply?

VERNON   So do we.

HOTSPUR   His is certain, ours is doubtful.

WORCESTER   Good cousin, be advis'd, stir not to-night.

VERNON   Do not, my lord.

DOUGLAS   You do not counsel well,
    You speak it out of fear, and cold heart.

VERNON   Do me no slander, Douglas; by my life,
    And I dare well maintain it with my life,

If well-respected honour bid me on,
I hold as little counsel with weak fear
As you, my lord, or any Scot that this day lives:
Let it be seen to-morrow in the battle
Which of us fears.

DOUGLAS   Yea, or to-night.

VERNON   Content.

HOTSPUR   To-night, say I.

VERNON   Come, come, it may not be. I wonder much,
Being men of such great leading as you are,
That you foresee not what impediments
Drag back our expedition: certain horse
Of my cousin Vernon's are not yet come up:
Your uncle Worcester's horse came but to-day,
And now their pride and mettle is asleep,
Their courage with hard labour tame and dull,
That not a horse is half the half of himself.

HOTSPUR   So are the horses of the enemy.
In general journey bated and brought low;
The better part of ours are full of rest.

WORCESTER   The number of the king exceedeth ours;
For God's sake, cousin, stay till all come in.

[*The trumpet sounds a parley*]

Enter Sir Walter Blunt

BLUNT   I come with gracious offers from the king,
If you vouchsafe me hearing and respect.

HOTSPUR   Welcome, Sir Walter Blunt; and would to God
You were of our determination!
Some of us love you well, and even those some
Envy your great deservings and good name,
Because you are not of our quality,
But stand against us like an enemy.

BLUNT   And God defend but still I should stand so,
So long as out of limit and true rule
You stand against anointed majesty.

But to my charge. The king hath sent to know
The nature of your griefs, and whereupon
You conjure from the breast of civil peace
Such bold hostility, teaching his duteous land
Audacious cruelty. If that the king
Have any way your good deserts forgot,
Which he confesseth to be manifold,
He bids you name your griefs, and with all speed
You shall have your desires with interest,
And pardon absolute for yourself, and these
Herein misled by your suggestion.

HOTSPUR The king is kind, and well we know the king
Knows at what time to promise, when to pay.
My father, and my uncle, and myself
Did give him that same royalty he wears,
And when he was not six and twenty strong,
Sick in the world's regard, wretched and low,
A poor unminded outlaw sneaking home,
My father gave him welcome to the shore,
And when he heard him swear and vow to God
He came but to be Duke of Lancaster,
To sue his livery, and beg his peace,
With tears of innocency, and terms of zeal,
My father, in kind heart and pity mov'd,
Swore him assistance, and perform'd it too.
Now when the lords and barons of the realm
Perceiv'd Northumberland did lean to him,
The more and less came in with cap and knee,
Met him in boroughs, cities, villages,
Attended him on bridges, stood in lanes,
Laid gifts before him, proffer'd him their oaths,
Gave him their heirs, as pages follow'd him,
Even at the heels, in golden multitudes.
He presently, as greatness knows itself,
Steps me a little higher than his vow
Made to my father while his blood was poor,

Upon the naked shore at Ravenspurgh,
And now forsooth takes on him to reform
Some certain edicts, and some strait decrees,
That lie too heavy on the commonwealth,
Cries out upon abuses, seems to weep
Over his country's wrongs, and by this face,
This seeming brow of justice, did he win
The hearts of all that he did angle for:
Proceeded further, cut me off the heads
Of all the favourites that the absent king
In deputation left behind him here,
When he was personal in the Irish war.
BLUNT   Tut, I came not to hear this.
HOTSPUR   Then to the point.
In short time after he depos'd the king,
Soon after that, depriv'd him of his life,
And in the neck of that, task'd the whole state,
To make that worse, suffer'd his kinsman March,
(Who is, if every owner were well plac'd,
Indeed his king), to be engag'd in Wales,
There without ransom to lie forfeited,
Disgrac'd me in my happy victories,
Sought to entrap me by intelligence,
Rated mine uncle from the council-board,
In rage dismiss'd my father from the court,
Broke oath on oath, committed wrong on wrong,
And in conclusion drove us to seek out
This head of safety, and withal to pry
Into his title, the which we find
Too indirect for long continuance.
BLUNT   Shall I return this answer to the king?
HOTSPUR   Not so, Sir Walter: we'll withdraw a while.
Go to the king, and let there be impawn'd
Some surety for a safe return again,
And in the morning early shall mine uncle
Bring him our purposes, and so farewell.

BLUNT   I would you would accept of grace and love.
HOTSPUR   And may be so we shall.
BLUNT   Pray God you do. [*Exeunt*]

Scene Four: **York. The Archbishop's Palace**

Enter the Archbishop of York and Sir Michael

ARCHBISHOP   Hie, good Sir Michael, bear this sealed brief
  With winged haste to the lord marshal,
  This to my cousin Scroop, and all the rest
  To whom they are directed. If you knew
  How much they do import, you would make haste.
MICHAEL   My good lord,
  I guess their tenour.
ARCHBISHOP   Like enough you do.
  To-morrow, good Sir Michael, is a day
  Wherein the fortune of ten thousand men
  Must bide the touch; for, sir, at Shrewsbury,
  As I am truly given to understand,
  The king with mighty and quick-raised power
  Meets with Lord Harry: and, I fear, Sir Michael,
  What with the sickness of Northumberland,
  Whose power was in the first proportion,
  And what with Owen Glendower's absence thence,
  Who with them was a rated sinew too,
  And comes not in, o'er-ruled by prophecies,
  I fear the power of Percy is too weak
  To wage an instant trial with the king.
MICHAEL   Why, my good lord, you need not fear;
  There is Douglas, and Lord Mortimer.
ARCHBISHOP   No, Mortimer is not there.
MICHAEL   But there is Mordake, Vernon, Lord Harry Percy,
  And there is my Lord of Worcester, and a head
  Of gallant warriors, noble gentlemen.

ARCHBISHOP   And so there is: but yet the king hath drawn
    The special head of all the land together,
    The Prince of Wales, Lord John of Lancaster,
    The noble Westmoreland and warlike Blunt,
    And many moe corivals and dear men
    Of estimation and command in arms.
MICHAEL   Doubt not, my lord, they shall be well oppos'd.
ARCHBISHOP   I hope no less, yet needful 'tis to fear;
    And, to prevent the worst, Sir Michael, speed:
    For if Lord Percy thrive not, ere the king
    Dismiss his power, he means to visit us,
    For he hath heard of our confederacy,
    And 'tis but wisdom to make strong against him:
    Therefore make haste; I must go write again
    To other friends, and so farewell, Sir Michael.   [*Exeunt*]

ACT FIFTH

Scene One: **The King's Camp near Shrewsbury**

Enter the King, the Prince of Wales, Lord John of Lancaster, Sir Walter Blunt, and Falstaff

KING   How bloodily the sun begins to peer
Above yon busky hill! the day looks pale
At his distemperature.
PRINCE   The southern wind
Doth play the trumpet to his purposes,
And by his hollow whistling in the leaves
Foretells a tempest and a blustering day.
KING   Then with the losers let it sympathize,
For nothing can seem foul to those that win.

[*The trumpet sounds*]

Enter Worcester and Vernon

How now, my Lord of Worcester? 'tis not well
That you and I should meet upon such terms
As now we meet. You have deceiv'd our trust,
And made us doff our easy robes of peace,
To crush our old limbs in ungentle steel:
This is not well, my lord, this is not well.
What say you to it? will you again unknit
This churlish knot of all-abhorred war?
And move in that obedient orb again
Where you did give a fair and natural light,
And be no more an exhal'd meteor,
A prodigy of fear, and a portent
Of broached mischief to the unborn times?
WORCESTER   Hear me, my liege:
For mine own part, I could be well content
To entertain the lag-end of my life

With quiet hours; for, I protest,
I have not sought the day of this dislike.
KING   You have not sought it? how comes it, then?
FALSTAFF   Rebellion lay in his way, and he found it.
PRINCE   Peace, chewet, peace!
WORCESTER   It pleas'd your majesty to turn your looks
Of favour from myself, and all our house;
And yet I must remember you, my lord,
We were the first and dearest of your friends.
For you my staff of office did I break
In Richard's time, and posted day and night
To meet you on the way, and kiss your hand,
When yet you were in place, and in account,
Nothing so strong and fortunate as I.
It was myself, my brother, and his son,
That brought you home, and boldly did outdare
The dangers of the time. You swore to us,
And you did swear that oath at Doncaster,
That you did nothing purpose 'gainst the state,
Nor claim no further than your new-fall'n right,
The seat of Gaunt, dukedom of Lancaster:
To this we swore our aid. But in short space
It rain'd down fortune showering on your head,
And such a flood of greatness fell on you,
What with our help, what with the absent king,
What with the injuries of a wanton time,
The seeming sufferances that you had borne,
And the contrarious winds that held the king
So long in his unlucky Irish wars,
That all in England did repute him dead:
And from this swarm of fair advantages
You took occasion to be quickly woo'd
To gripe the general sway into your hand,
Forgot your oath to us at Doncaster,
And being fed by us you us'd us so
As that ungentle gull, the cuckoo's bird,

Useth the sparrow, did oppress our nest,
Grew by our feeding to so great a bulk
That even our love durst not come near your sight,
For fear of swallowing; but with nimble wing
We were enforc'd, for safety sake, to fly
Out of your sight, and raise this present head,
Whereby we stand opposed by such means
As you yourself have forg'd against yourself,
By unkind usage, dangerous countenance,
And violation of all faith and troth,
Sworn to us in your younger enterprise.

KING   These things indeed you have articulate,
Proclaim'd at market crosses, read in churches,
To face the garment of rebellion
With some fine colour that may please the eye
Of fickle changelings and poor discontents,
Which gape and rub the elbow at the news
Of hurlyburly innovation;
And never yet did insurrection want
Such water-colours to impaint his cause,
Nor moody beggars, starving for a time
Of pellmell havoc and confusion.

PRINCE   In both your armies there is many a soul
Shall pay full dearly for this encounter,
If once they join in trial. Tell your nephew,
The Prince of Wales doth join with all the world
In praise of Henry Percy: by my hopes,
This present enterprise set off his head,
I do not think a braver gentleman,
More active, valiant, or more valiant young,
More daring, or more bold, is now alive
To grace this latter age with noble deeds.
For my part, I may speak it to my shame,
I have a truant been to chivalry,
And so I hear he doth account me too;
Yet this before my father's majesty—

91

I am content that he shall take the odds
Of his great name and estimation,
And will, to save the blood on either side,
Try fortune with him in a single fight.
KING   And, Prince of Wales, so dare we venture thee,
Albeit considerations infinite
Do make against it. No, good Worcester, no,
We love our people well, even those we love
That are misled upon your cousin's part,
And, will they take the offer of our grace,
Both he, and they, and you, yea, every man
Shall be my friend again, and I'll be his:
So tell your cousin, and bring me word
What he will do. But if he will not yield,
Rebuke and dread correction wait on us,
And they shall do their office. So, be gone;
We will not now be troubled with reply:
We offer fair; take it advisedly.   [*Exeunt Worcester and Vernon*]
PRINCE   It will not be accepted, on my life;
The Douglas and the Hotspur both together
Are confident against the world in arms.
KING   Hence, therefore, every leader to his charge,
For on their answer will we set on them,
And God befriend us as our cause is just!
                    [*Exeunt all but the Prince of Wales and Falstaff*]
FALSTAFF   Hal, if thou see me down in the battle, and bestride
me, so, 'tis a point of friendship.
PRINCE   Nothing but a colossus can do thee that friendship.
Say thy prayers, and farewell.
FALSTAFF   I would 'twere bed-time, Hal, and all well.
PRINCE   Why, thou owest God a death.   [*Exit*]
FALSTAFF   'Tis not due yet, I would be loath to pay him before
his day, what need I be so forward with him that calls not on
me? Well, 'tis no matter, honour pricks me on, yea, but how if
honour prick me off when I come on? How then? can honour
set to a leg? no: or an arm? no: or take away the grief of a

Glendower

wound? no. Honour hath no skill in surgery, then? no. What is honour? a word; what is in that word honour? what is that honour? air. A trim reckoning! Who hath it? he that died o' Wednesday. Doth he feel it? no. Doth he hear it? no. 'Tis insensible, then? yea, to the dead. But will it not live with the living? no. Why? detraction will not suffer it, therefore I'll none of it, honour is a mere scutcheon, and so ends my cate-chism.   [*Exit*]

Scene Two: **The Rebel Camp**

Enter Worcester and Vernon

WORCESTER   O, no, my nephew must not know, Sir Richard,
The liberal and kind offer of the king.
VERNON   'Twere best he did.
WORCESTER   Then are we all undone.
It is not possible, it cannot be,
The king should keep his word in loving us;
He will suspect us still, and find a time
To punish this offence in other faults:
Suspicion all our lives shall be stuck full of eyes,
For treason is but trusted like the fox,
Who, ne'er so tame, so cherish'd and lock'd up,
Will have a wild trick of his ancestors.
Look how we can, or sad or merrily,
Interpretation will misquote our looks,
And we shall feed like oxen at a stall,
The better cherish'd still the nearer death;
My nephew's trespass may be well forgot,
It hath the excuse of youth and heat of blood,
And an adopted name of privilege,
A hare-brain'd Hotspur govern'd by a spleen;
All his offences live upon my head
And on his father's; we did train him on,
And, his corruption being ta'en from us,

We, as the spring of all, shall pay for all.
Therefore, good cousin, let not Harry know,
In any case, the offer of the king.

VERNON   Deliver what you will, I'll say 'tis so.
Here comes your cousin.

Enter Hotspur and Douglas

HOTSPUR   My uncle is return'd;
Deliver up my Lord of Westmoreland,
Uncle, what news?

WORCESTER   The king will bid you battle presently.

DOUGLAS   Defy him by the Lord of Westmoreland.

HOTSPUR   Lord Douglas, go you and tell him so.

DOUGLAS   Marry, and shall, and very willingly.   [*Exit*]

WORCESTER   There is no seeming mercy in the king.

HOTSPUR   Did you beg any? God forbid!

WORCESTER   I told him gently of our grievances,
Of his oath-breaking, which he mended thus,
By now forswearing that he is forsworn:
He calls us rebels, traitors, and will scourge
With haughty arms this hateful name in us.

Re-enter Douglas

DOUGLAS   Arm, gentlemen, to arms! for I have thrown
A brave defiance in King Henry's teeth,
And Westmoreland, that was engag'd, did bear it,
Which cannot choose but bring him quickly on.

WORCESTER   The Prince of Wales stepp'd forth before the
king,
And, nephew, challeng'd you to single fight.

HOTSPUR   O, would the quarrel lay upon our heads,
And that no man might draw short breath to-day
But I and Harry Monmouth! Tell me, tell me,
How show'd his tasking? seem'd it in contempt?

VERNON   No, by my soul, I never in my life
Did hear a challenge urg'd more modestly,

94

Unless a brother should a brother dare
To gentle exercise and proof of arms.
He gave you all the duties of a man,
Trimm'd up your praises with a princely tongue,
Spoke your deservings like a chronicle,
Making you ever better than his praise
By still dispraising praise valued with you,
And, which became him like a prince indeed,
He made a blushing cital of himself,
And chid his truant youth with such a grace
As if he master'd there a double spirit
Of teaching and of learning instantly.
There did he pause; but let me tell the world,
If he outlive the envy of this day,
England did never owe so sweet a hope,
So much misconstrued in his wantonness.

HOTSPUR   Cousin, I think thou art enamoured
On his follies: never did I hear
Of any prince so wild a liberty.
But be he as he will, yet once ere night
I will embrace him with a soldier's arm,
That he shall shrink under my courtesy.
Arm, arm with speed, and, fellows, soldiers, friends,
Better consider what you have to do
Than I, that have not well the gift of tongue,
Can lift your blood up with persuasion.

Enter a Messenger

MESSENGER   My lord, here are letters for you.
HOTSPUR   I cannot read them now;
O gentlemen, the time of life is short,
To spend that shortness basely were too long,
If life did ride upon a dial's point,
Still ending at the arrival of an hour;
An if we live, we live to tread on kings,
If die, brave death, when princes die with us!

Now, for our consciences, the arms are fair,
When the intent of bearing them is just.

Enter another Messenger

MESSENGER   My lord, prepare, the king comes on apace.
HOTSPUR   I thank him that he cuts me from my tale,
For I profess not talking; only this—
Let each man do his best: and here draw I
A sword, whose temper I intend to stain
With the best blood that I can meet withal
In the adventure of this perilous day.
Now, Esperance! Percy! and set on!
Sound all the lofty instruments of war,
And by that music let us all embrace,
For, heaven to earth, some of us never shall
A second time do such a courtesy.

> [*The trumpets sound. They embrace, and exeunt*]

Scenes Three, Four and Five: **Plain between the camps**

*The King enters with his power, Alarum to the battle. Then enter
Douglas and Sir Walter Blunt*

BLUNT   What is thy name, that in the battle thus
Thou crossest me? what honour dost thou seek
Upon my head?
DOUGLAS   Know then, my name is Douglas;
And I do haunt thee in the battle thus,
Because some tell me that thou art a king.
BLUNT   They tell thee true.
DOUGLAS   The Lord of Stafford dear to-day hath bought
Thy likeness, for instead of thee, King Harry,
This sword hath ended him: so shall it thee,
Unless thou yield thee as my prisoner.
BLUNT   I was not born a yielder, thou proud Scot;

And thou shalt find a king that will revenge
Lord Stafford's death.

[They fight. Douglas kills Blunt]

Enter Hotspur

HOTSPUR O Douglas, hadst thou fought at Holmedon thus,
I never had triumph'd upon a Scot.
DOUGLAS All's done, all's won; here breathless lies the king.
HOTSPUR Where?
DOUGLAS Here.
HOTSPUR This, Douglas? no: I know this face full well:
A gallant knight he was, his name was Blunt,
Semblably furnish'd like the king himself.
DOUGLAS A fool go with thy soul, whither it goes!
A borrow'd title hast thou bought too dear:
Why didst thou tell me that thou wert a king?
HOTSPUR The king hath many marching in his coats.
DOUGLAS Now, by my sword, I will kill all his coats;
I'll murder all his wardrobe, piece by piece,
Until I meet the king.
HOTSPUR   Up, and away!
Our soldiers stand full fairly for the day.   *[Exeunt]*

Alarum. Enter Falstaff, solus

FALSTAFF Though I could 'scape shot-free at London, I fear
the shot here, here's no scoring but upon the pate. Soft, who
are you? Sir Walter Blunt, there's honour for you, here's no
vanity; I am as hot as molten lead, and as heavy too: God keep
lead out of me, I need no more weight than mine own bowels.
I have led my ragamuffins where they are pepper'd, there's
not three of my hundred and fifty left alive, and they are for
the town's end, to beg during life. But who comes here?

Enter the Prince

PRINCE What, stand'st thou idle here? lend me thy sword:
Many a noble man lies stark and stiff

97

Under the hoofs of vaunting enemies,
Whose deaths are yet unreveng'd: I prithee lend me thy sword.

FALSTAFF   O Hal, I prithee give me leave to breathe a while;
Turk Gregory never did such deeds in arms as I have done this
day, I have paid Percy, I have made him sure.

PRINCE   He is, indeed; and living to kill thee.
I prithee lend me thy sword.

FALSTAFF   Nay, before God, Hal, if Percy be alive, thou get'st
not my sword, but take my pistol, if thou wilt.

PRINCE   Give it me: what, is it in the case?

FALSTAFF   Ay, Hal, 'tis hot, 'tis hot, there's that will sack a city.
[*The Prince draws it out, and finds it to be a bottle of sack*]

PRINCE   What, is it a time to jest and dally now?
[*He throws the bottle at him. Exit*]

FALSTAFF   Well, if Percy be alive, I'll pierce him. If he do come
in my way, so; if he do not, if I come in his willingly, let him
make a carbonado of me. I like not such grinning honour as
Sir Walter hath, give me life, which if I can save, so; if not,
honour comes unlook'd for, and there's an end.   [*Exit*]

*Alarum. Excursions. Enter the King, the Prince, Lord John of
Lancaster, and Earl of Westmoreland*

KING   I prithee,
Harry, withdraw thyself; thou bleed'st too much.
Lord John of Lancaster, go you with him.

LANCASTER   Not I, my lord, unless I did bleed too.

PRINCE   I beseech your majesty, make up,
Lest your retirement do amaze your friends.

KING   I will do so.
My Lord of Westmoreland, lead him to his tent.

WESTMORELAND   Come, my lord, I'll lead you to your tent.

PRINCE   Lead me, my lord? I do not need your help:
And God forbid a shallow scratch should drive
The Prince of Wales from such a field as this,
Where stain'd nobility lies trodden on,
And rebels' arms triumph in massacres!

LANCASTER We breathe too long, come, cousin Westmoreland,
  Our duty this way lies; for God's sake, come.
                    [*Exeunt Prince John and Westmoreland*]
PRINCE By God, thou hast deceiv'd me, Lancaster,
  I did not think thee lord of such a spirit;
  Before, I loved thee as a brother, John,
  But now, I do respect thee as my soul.
KING I saw him hold Lord Percy at the point,
  With lustier maintenance than I did look for
  Of such an ungrown warrior.
PRINCE   O, this boy
  Lends mettle to us all!   [*Exit*]

Enter Douglas

DOUGLAS Another king? they grow like Hydra's heads:
  I am the Douglas, fatal to all those
  That wear those colours on them: what art thou,
  That counterfeit'st the person of a king?
KING The king himself, who, Douglas, grieves at heart
  So many of his shadows thou hast met
  And not the very king. I have two boys
  Seek Percy and thyself about the field,
  But, seeing thou fall'st on me so luckily,
  I will assay thee, and defend thyself.
DOUGLAS I fear thou art another counterfeit,
  And yet, in faith, thou bear'st thee like a king,
  But mine I am sure thou art, whoe'er thou be,
  And thus I win thee.
        [*They fight; the King being in danger, re-enter Prince of Wales*]
PRINCE Hold up thy head, vile Scot, or thou art like
  Never to hold it up again! the spirits
  Of valiant Shirley, Stafford, Blunt, are in my arms,
  It is the Prince of Wales that threatens thee,
  Who never promiseth but he means to pay.
                        [*They fight; Douglas flies*]
  Cheerly, my lord, how fares your grace?

Sir Nicholas Gawsey hath for succour sent,
And so hath Clifton; I'll to Clifton straight.
KING   Stay, and breathe awhile:
Thou hast redeem'd thy lost opinion,
And show'd thou mak'st some tender of my life,
In this fair rescue thou hast brought to me.
PRINCE   O God, they did me too much injury
That ever said I hearken'd for your death;
If it were so, I might have let alone
The insulting hand of Douglas over you,
Which would have been as speedy in your end
As all the poisonous potions in the world,
And saved the treacherous labour of your son.
KING   Make up to Clifton: I'll to Sir Nicholas Gawsey.   [*Exit*]

Enter Hotspur

HOTSPUR   If I mistake not, thou art Harry Monmouth.
PRINCE   Thou speak'st as if I would deny my name.
HOTSPUR   My name is Harry Percy.
PRINCE   Why, then I see
A very valiant rebel of the name;
I am the Prince of Wales, and think not, Percy,
To share with me in glory any more:
Two stars keep not their motion in one sphere,
Nor can one England brook a double reign,
Of Harry Percy and the Prince of Wales.
HOTSPUR   Nor shall it, Harry, for the hour is come
To end the one of us, and would to God
Thy name in arms were now as great as mine!
PRINCE   I'll make it greater ere I part from thee,
And all the budding honours on thy crest
I'll crop to make a garland for my head.
HOTSPUR   I can no longer brook thy vanities.   [*They fight*]

Enter Falstaff

FALSTAFF   Well said, Hal! to it, Hal! Nay, you shall find no
boy's play here, I can tell you.

Re-enter Douglas; he fights with Falstaff, who falls down as if he
were dead, and exit Douglas. Hotspur is wounded, and falls

HOTSPUR   O, Harry, thou hast robb'd me of my youth;
I better brook the loss of brittle life
Than those proud titles thou hast won of me;
They wound my thoughts worse than thy sword my flesh,
But thoughts the slaves of life, and life time's fool,
And time, that takes survey of all the world,
Must have a stop. O, I could prophesy,
But that the earthy and cold hand of death
Lies on my tongue: no, Percy, thou art dust,
And food for—   [*Dies*]
PRINCE   For worms, brave Percy: fare thee well, great heart!
Ill-weav'd ambition, how much art thou shrunk!
When that this body did contain a spirit,
A kingdom for it was too small a bound,
But now two paces of the vilest earth
Is room enough: this earth that bears thee dead
Bears not alive so stout a gentleman;
If thou wert sensible of courtesy,
I should not make so dear a show of zeal,
But let my favours hide thy mangled face,
And, even in thy behalf, I'll thank myself
For doing these fair rites of tenderness;
Adieu, and take thy praise with thee to heaven,
Thy ignominy sleep with thee in the grave,
But not remember'd in thy epitaph!
                          [*He spieth Falstaff on the ground*]
What, old acquaintance, could not all this flesh
Keep in a little life? Poor Jack, farewell;
I could have better spar'd a better man:
O, I should have a heavy miss of thee,
If I were much in love with vanity!

Death hath not struck so fat a deer to-day,
Though many dearer, in this bloody fray.
Embowell'd will I see thee by and by:
Till then in blood by noble Percy lie.   *[Exit]*

FALSTAFF (*rising up*) Embowelled? if thou embowel me to-day,
I'll give you leave to powder me and eat me too to-morrow.
'Sblood, 'twas time to counterfeit, or that hot termagant Scot
had paid me scot and lot too. Counterfeit? I lie, I am no
counterfeit, to die is to be a counterfeit, for he is but the counterfeit of a man who hath not the life of a man: but to counterfeit dying when a man thereby liveth, is to be no counterfeit,
but the true and perfect image of life indeed. The better part of
valour is discretion, in the which better part I have saved my
life. 'Zounds, I am afraid of this gunpowder Percy, though he
be dead, how if he should counterfeit too and rise? by my faith,
I am afraid he would prove the better counterfeit, therefore I'll
make him sure, yea, and I'll swear I kill'd him. Why may he
not rise as well as I? Nothing confutes me but eyes, and nobody
sees me. Therefore, sirrah (*stabbing him*), with a new wound in
your thigh, come you along with me.
                              [*Takes up Hotspur on his back*]

Re-enter the Prince of Wales and Lord John of Lancaster

PRINCE   Come, brother John; full bravely hast thou flesh'd
Thy maiden sword.
LANCASTER   But, soft! whom have we here?
Did you not tell me this fat man was dead?
PRINCE   I did, I saw him dead,
Breathless and bleeding on the ground. Art thou alive?
Or is it fantasy that plays upon our eyesight?
I prithee speak, we will not trust our eyes
Without our ears, thou art not what thou seem'st.
FALSTAFF   No, that's certain, I am not a double man: but if I
be not Jack Falstaff, then am I a Jack. There is Percy (*throwing
the body down*): if your father will do me any honour, so; if not,
let him kill the next Percy himself. I look to be either earl or
duke, I can assure you.

PRINCE   Why, Percy I kill'd myself, and saw thee dead.

FALSTAFF   Didst thou? Lord, Lord, how this world is given to lying! I grant you I was down, and out of breath, and so was he, but we rose both at an instant, and fought a long hour by Shrewsbury clock; if I may be believ'd, so; if not, let them that should reward valour bear the sin upon their own heads. I'll take it upon my death, I gave him this wound in the thigh: if the man were alive, and would deny it, 'zounds, I would make him eat a piece of my sword.

LANCASTER   This is the strangest tale that ever I heard.

PRINCE   This is the strangest fellow, brother John.
Come, bring your luggage nobly on your back:
For my part, if a lie may do thee grace,
I'll gild it with the happiest terms I have. [*A retreat is sounded*]
The trumpet sounds retreat, the day is ours.
Come, brother, let us to the highest of the field,
To see what friends are living, who are dead.
　　　　　　　　　　　　[*Exeunt Prince of Wales and Lancaster*]

FALSTAFF   I'll follow, as they say, for reward. He that rewards me, God reward him! If I do grow great, I'll grow less, for I'll purge, and leave sack, and live cleanly as a nobleman should do.
　　　　　　　　　　　　　　　　　　　　　　　　　[*Exit*]

The trumpets sound. Enter the King, Prince of Wales, Lord John of Lancaster, Earl of Westmoreland, with Worcester and Vernon prisoners

KING   Thus ever did rebellion find rebuke.
Ill-spirited Worcester, did not we send grace,
Pardon, and terms of love to all of you?
And wouldst thou turn our offers contrary?
Misuse the tenour of thy kinsman's trust?
Three knights upon our party slain to-day,
A noble earl and many a creature else,
Had been alive this hour,
If like a Christian thou hadst truly borne
Betwixt our armies true intelligence.

WORCESTER   What I have done my safety urg'd me to;
And I embrace this fortune patiently,
Since not to be avoided it falls on me.
KING   Bear Worcester to the death, and Vernon too:
Other offenders we will pause upon.
                              [*Exeunt Worcester and Vernon, guarded*]
How goes the field?
PRINCE   The noble Scot, Lord Douglas, when he saw
The fortune of the day quite turn'd from him,
The noble Percy slain, and all his men
Upon the foot of fear, fled with the rest,
And falling from a hill, he was so bruis'd
That the pursuers took him. At my tent
The Douglas is; and I beseech your grace
I may dispose of him.
KING   With all my heart.
PRINCE   Then, brother John of Lancaster, to you
This honourable bounty shall belong:
Go to the Douglas, and deliver him
Up to his pleasure, ransomless and free:
His valour shown upon our crests to-day
Hath taught us how to cherish such high deeds
Even in the bosom of our adversaries.
LANCASTER   I thank your grace for this high courtesy,
Which I shall give away immediately.
KING   Then this remains, that we divide our power.
You, son John, and my cousin Westmoreland
Towards York shall bend you with your dearest speed,
To meet Northumberland and the prelate Scroop,
Who, as we hear, are busily in arms:
Myself and you, son Harry, will towards Wales,
To fight with Glendower and the Earl of March.
Rebellion in this land shall lose his sway,
Meeting the check of such another day,
And since this business so fair is done,
Let us not leave till all our own be won.   [*Exeunt*]

GLOSSARY

The words are given only the meanings which they bear in their present context.—J.R.

Act I, Scene 1

Act I, Scene 2

Act I, Scene 3

Act II, Scene 1

Act II, Scene 2

Act II, Scene 3

Act II, Scene 4

69 *start,* sudden fit
  favours, features
70 *factor,* agent

engross, store up
advertisement, information

Act III, Scene 3

71 *bate,* lose weight
  liking, good condition
  compass, limits
72 *ignis fatuus,* will o' wisp
  links, tortures
73 *Dowlas,* coarse linen
  bolters, cloth for sifting meal
  holland, fine lawn

by-drinkings, odd drinks
denier, tenth of a sou
younker, greenhorn
door, quarter
74 *stew'd prune,* prostitute
  ought, owed
75 *emboss'd,* swollen
75 *furniture,* equipment

Act IV, Scene 1

77 *soothers,* flatterers
  approve, test
  justling, hectic
78 *advertisement,* advice
  main } main chance
       } army
  nice, precarious
  list, limit
  reversion, prospect of inherit-
       ance

hair, nature
79 *offering,* attacking
  strict, critical
80 *daff'd,* tossed
  estridges, goshawks
80 *with . . . Baited,* beat their
       wings in the wind
  beaver, helmet
  cuisses, armour
  wind, wheel about

Act IV, Scene 2

Act V, Scene 2

Act V, Scenes 3, 4 and 5